YEADON'S REGISTER

of

L N E R

LOCOMOTIVES

Volume Seven

B12 CLASS

Copyright Booklaw/Railbus 2001
ISBN 1 899 624 67 8

DEDICATION

To Annie and Jean
who both know where, and how well,
another B12 is still working.

*The Yeadon Collection is available for inspection and anyone who wishes to
inspect it should contact:-*
The Archivist
Brynmor Jones Library
University of Hull
Hull
HU6 7RX
Tel: 01482-465265
A catalogue of the Yeadon collection is available.

First published in the United Kingdom by Irwell Press
Reprinted by BOOKLAW/RAILBUS 2001 in association with CHALLENGER
382 Carlton Hill, Nottingham NG4 1JA
www.booklawpublications.co.uk
Printed and bound by The Amadeus Press, Cleckheaton.

CLASS B12

INTRODUCTION

The working life of this class spanned almost 50 years, from December 1911 until September 1961, and all maintenance was done either at Stratford or at Inverurie Works. Living in Hull, and employed very full time designing and selling mechanical power transmission equipment, opportunity, distance, and cost conspired so that it was impossible to establish the necessary rapport to get the complete detailed information as to dates of works visits to match what I was able to achieve at Doncaster, Darlington, and Gorton Works.

That deficiency was not improved by the circumstances which obtained at those works in London and in Aberdeenshire. At Stratford, repairs could take place in either the 'New' (c.1921) or 'Old' Works, and quite separate records were kept by each. Luckily, I did get considerable documentation from the latter, but was never able to "make my number" in the New Works, and it was there that repairs to the B12 class were done. That could have been circumvented had I obtained the Record of Locomotive sheets *ref. C.M.E. 9018* for copying when Stratford ceased to repair steam locomotives early in 1960. By the time that I was able to visit the Works Manager's office to ask about them, they were no longer in their possession. Despite a widespread and lengthy search they have never been located, to my disappointment and great regret.

Beginning in April 1931, no less than 25 of the class of 80 B12s were sent to work as far away from Stratford as it was possible to do on the LNER. They became Northern Scottish Area allocated engines, and the works at Inverurie took over their maintenance, and the recording of repairs done to them. To make personal contact there involved a round trip (by rail) of 789 miles, needing serious consideration of cost, and time. On the rare occasions when I could arrange for their provenance to coincide, the Inverurie office staff courteously extended to me such detailed data as they could find, but it was only complete from about 1944.

Clearly the wartime re-cycling of paper, or rigorous disposal for salvage, had been applied to the earlier material. However, Boiler Shop records did provide dates for all boiler changes, and for general repairs, thus producing those of real significance. Later, at the Scottish Record Office in Edinburgh, the Assistant Keeper, George Barbour (a dedicated enthusiast for railways) guided me to some additional material which enabled light repairs at Inverurie for the mid-1930s to be added. Curiously, they only gave the date ex-works, and their frequency showed how dependent that small self-contained region of the LNER was on the works for even minor repairs, such as would normally have been done at district level in the bigger Areas.

Despite making every effort that I could think of over the past 40 years, Volume 7 thus fails to furnish the complete coverage included hitherto. Some 25 years membership of the G N S R Association (admittedly at long range) has not led to filling the gaps from their archives, nor contact with anyone having acquired from Inverurie information which I lack. Equally, the Great Eastern Railway Society have informed me that they do not have the C.M.E. 9018 sheets on which Stratford entered dates of works visits for repairs. I would thus be only too happy to do an up-graded edition of this *Register*

8509 as turned out from Stratford in May 1929 after removal of the Worthington feed water heater, could have been expected to have had its number on cab side instead of tender, a change made general in February 1929. It has the vacuum brake added, and a coal guard on tender. Sanding was provided for both directions of running and was compressed air operated.

The drive to the Lentz poppet valves is clearly visible on 8516 in this view ex-works in January 1928. When they were fitted in November 1926, the hitherto power operated reversing gear was changed to screw operation. Coal guard and vacuum brake additions show up well, as does the coach heating hose at front end.

should any reader be able to contribute something to filling the gaps in this current one.

REGISTRATION

My acquaintance with the B12 class had to be sought by extensive travelling for only two were recorded at Hull, the first in 1925 when 1561E was on Doncaster shed's triangular working to York, thence Hull, and back to Doncaster. We did not see one here again until May 1959 when 61577 limped in from Bridlington after a special working. Nevertheless, I did manage to meet up with all except 8534, the first of the eighty LNER engines to be scrapped, in June 1945. From recording 8507 at Stratford shed on May 8th 1937, it took until August 18th 1949 to log the last one, 61513, at Kittybrewster shed. In between, I did manage to see 7472, 7482, 7488, and 7491 in that short-lived renumbering.

Opportunities to be hauled by a B12 rarely came my way, but I did ride behind Parts 1, 3, and 4, the poppet-valved Part 2 becoming extinct in January 1934. Runs with Part 1 locos concerned 8532, 1548, and 61543, and 61507 was a Part 4 when it took me from Aberdeen to Ballater and back in August 1949. My nine Part 3s were 8509, 1514, 1519, 1535, 1538, 1558, E1510, 61553 and 61577. On the G.E. lines they took me Cambridge - Ipswich, Ipswich - Harwich Town, Liverpool Street - Ipswich, and Liverpool Street - Southend, the latter bringing further reward by seeing the Australian cricket team score 721 runs in that Saturday's 6 hours play against Essex, of which Bradman's share was 185 - small beer against the two 300s I saw him make in Test matches at Headingley in 1930 and 1934.

Not often is it realised that this class worked in some unusual places far away from the G.E. and the Northern Scottish Area. In the 1920s they regularly worked the *North Country Continental* boat train to and from Manchester (Central), and from 1949, Grantham shed was home to some of them, almost to the end of the class. But

on my first visit to Eastfield shed in Glasgow on July 17th 1937, I had the surprised pleasure of seeing not only 8503 but also 8548, there to work summer excursions to Fort William and Oban, using the 12-coach sets of green and cream painted open tourist stock. Then there were other surprises - 8521 going light through Galashiels on July 25th 1943, and 8548 on the pick-up goods at Helensburgh on August 4th 1943. War conditions had reduced the need for some of them to work north of Aberdeen, and Southern Scottish Area could use them to better advantage. As early in the war as March 1940 No.8526 went south to St Margarets in Edinburgh, and in the following December 8504 and 8543 went to Eastfield in Glasgow. A year later Haymarket got 8500 and 8503, followed in February 1942 by 8511 and 8521. In early 1943 Eastfield also took in 8502 and 8531, and in March Haymarket passed on 8500, 8503 and 8521 to St Margarets. Although their move south was spread over three years, all nine were called back north to Kittybrewster between August 18th and mid-September 1943. Under the heading "Now it can be told" (used by the LNER for a booklet on some of its wartime activities) it would be fascinating to learn what war work these B12s did whilst they were Edinburgh and Glasgow residents. With the U.S.A. jolted into active participation through Pearl Harbour in December 1941, of the four which then went south - were they for moving U.S. troops which began to arrive at ports on the Clyde? Another possibility could have been trains distributing Italian prisoners-of-war, of which considerable numbers arrived in this country. I well remember being in Waverley station in July 1941 and seeing hundreds of them come off a train, and marching off along Princes Street. My closest railway friend, the late Ron Copeman, was in command of a large batch of them in a camp at Rhu on the West Highland line, and Eastfield B12s could very well have been used to take them there.

61577's May 1959 Hull visit was entirely unforeseen. It had hauled a special train for the Institution of Water Engineers from

Lincoln to Driffield, and then proceeded to Bridlington shed to be serviced and prepared for the return working. There it was found to have run hot and to be unfit to risk on the special. So a B1 (actually 61377) was called up from Hull, and 61577 limped to Dairycoates shed for the needed attention. That shed then used it locally for a few days before returning it home to Cambridge. Luckily, this rare series of events was recorded by photographs of it working hard up hill at Enthorpe, on the special train, then at Bridlington shed alongside 61377, in Dairycoates shed, and in use on a pick-up goods at Hessle station. Literally, 61577 could claim that "I was a stranger, and you took me in, and ministered to me".

The low maximum axle loading of 15T 13C, stemming from their early G.E. limitations, proved to be a distinct bonus during the 1939-45 war. It enabled them to work heavy ambulance trains over many lines otherwise barred to engines with the necessary power. A tentative step was taken in October - December 1940 to give them wide availability, when 8519, 8538 and 8547 had their footsteps altered to give more clearance. Then in March/April 1944, as preparation for the Invasion of Europe and the anticipated heavy casualties, at least a dozen Part 3 examples were recorded as fitted with "ambulance valve", to make engine and train brakes compatible. Those engines were then based on Westbury, Newbury, and Templecombe, but for good security reasons, nothing about these moves was shown in the *Weekly Transfers*. In the summer of 1944 they ranged widely in the south and south-west of England, and were seen in very unlikely places.

NUMBERING

The Great Eastern Railway handed over 70 of this class to the LNER, numbered 1500-1505 and 1507-1570 - the missing 1506 had a life of only 4 months in 1913, being so badly damaged in a collision at Colchester that it was not worth repairing. Stratford cut up the remains in September 1913, though the boiler lived on to serve from August 1916 until July 1928, on five other engines of the class.

From February 1924 the LNER increased the engine numbers by seven thousand, so the 70 duly became 8500-5 and 8507-8570. To these, in 1928, were added a further ten engines, 8571-8580.

In 1942, as a wartime emergency job, Doncaster were building LMS 8F 2-8-0s which were to be numbered 8510-8539 in their se-

ries. To avoid any possible confusion, the B12s were to be renumbered 7415-7494. Stratford began that process with 8568 becoming 7482, and 8577 changing to 7491 on 31st October 1942. After 8574 was altered to 7488 on 23rd January 1943, those alterations ceased, and amongst the B12s were limited to eleven engines, viz: 7426, 7437, 7449, 7467, 7470, 7472, 7476, 7479, 7482, 7488 and 7491, all in Part 3 of the class. None of the engines which Inverurie maintained participated in the change of numbers. The eleven which changed then retained their 74XX numbers until the Thompson general renumbering of 1946, the series being cleared on 15th November when 7470 went to 1556. In the Thompson scheme, the class was allocated 1500-1505 and 1507-1570, all except the last ten (those constructed new in 1928) actually returning to their original Great Eastern numbers. A further unique feature was to continue the gap and in deference to 1506 the number remained blank. Only 8534, scrapped in June 1945, did not play a part in the 1946 renumbering.

Another curiosity of the B12 numbering occurred both after Grouping and also after Nationalisation. In the LNER's first attempt to differentiate between engines of the same number owned by its constituent companies, those maintained by Stratford were given an E suffix, 1516E, 1518E, 1534E, 1535E, 1536E, 1539E, 1542E, 1543E, 1544E, 1547E, 1561E, 1569E and 1570E all being so recorded. In early 1948, when British Railways faced a similar problem, they briefly employed a letter prefix on a Regional basis; B12s maintained at Stratford were in the Eastern Region, so were accorded an E prefix to their number, E1510, E1530, E1555, E1559 and E1567 being done in that style. By March 1948 the letter prefix was supplanted by a figure 6 for Eastern & N.E. Regions, so all B12 survivors then ended their career in 615XX numbering. Inverurie took no part in applying the Regional prefix letter, but put 615XX numbers on their B12s.

The Great Eastern also numbered its tenders to correspond with that of the engine to which they were first coupled - see the section on Tenders for further details. It was also Stratford's custom (until March 1914) to register a boiler with the same number as the running number of the engine on to which it was first fitted. But the economics of making boilers interchangeable halted that tidy arrangement. No.1564 was built in April 1920, and 1560 came new from Beardmore in May 1921, engines 1500 to 1564 first carrying

8533 was one of the six which Stratford altered from Part 1 to Part 2, but in February 1933 - as here - it lost the Lentz valves and reverted to Part 1. It did not acquire A.C.F.I. being re-boilered to Part 3 in 1937.

The original chimney had a copper cap, except on the 1928-built engines by which time most of the earlier locomotives had received a plain replacement. The cap on 8553 survived into the 1930s, but the steel ring on the smokebox door (see 8559 photo) was no longer being polished. Stratford made a sad job of moving the number from tender to cab side, throwing it out of alignment with the lettering on the tender, for which it also made the wrong choice of seven and a half inch size.

boilers numbered 1500 to 1564. Then the large 0-6-0 type (later to become LNER class J20) was designed to use the same boiler as the 4-6-0, and the coincidence of engine and boiler number ceased. In fact, the last six Stratford-built 4-6-0s were a real mish-mash; 1565 got boiler 1271, 1566 got boiler 1565, 1567 got 1273, 1568 got 1272, and the final two, 1569 and 1570, got boilers 3802 and 3803 in a new series altogether. The 1271, 1272, 1273 numbers were the same as the running numbers of 0-6-0s, whilst 3802 and 3803 were in a series that Stratford introduced in July 1919, and then continued to use until the British Railways boiler renumbering began in August 1950.

There was a slight hiccup in the switch to boilers having individual numbering, because the ten built by Beyer, Peacock in 1928 for engines 8571-8580 were given boilers. 1571-1580. Two of those, 1572 and 1574, were in use long enough to be renumbered by British Railways in 1951. The boiler diagram (LNER No.25) had a Belpaire firebox, and a total of 153 were built, used by classes B12/1, B12/2, and J20. Numbers were 1270-1274, 1285-1294, 1500-1565, 1571-1580, and 3800-3861, production ceasing in January 1931. Then from May 1932 came the change to 5ft., larger diameter boiler, with round-top firebox, to which the LNER gave Diagram No.99A, the engines fitted with it becoming B12/3 class. By July 1940 there were 65 boilers to that diagram, numbered 4100 to 4164, of which 50 survived to be renumbered 27900-27949 September 1950 to September 1953, the last of them going out of use when engine 61571 was withdrawn in January 1960. Rather surprisingly, British Railways built four more as late as September 1954/January 1955, numbered 27950-27953 and (fortunately for preservationists) 27950 is the boiler acquired with engine 61572 which, as yet, has had a working life of only 6 years.

Finally, from September 1942 to April 1947, the LNER built 30 boilers to their Diagram 25A, which was an up-dated version of the original, but with round-top firebox instead of Belpaire type. The first 25 were built by Doncaster, but the order for the final five was transferred to Stratford for building. Inverurie used them as replacements on the B12/1s which they maintained, rendering the engines B12/4 class, the others being used by Stratford to change Belpaire J20s to J20/1 with round-top firebox. These boilers were first allocated numbers 4450 to 4479, but the first 15 were fitted with Doncaster boiler numbers 9410-9424 instead of 4450-4464. Nine were sent to Northern Scottish Area, and were later allocated British Railways 23120-23128, but four were not fitted, for after subsequent transfer to Stratford, they took 23159, 23144, 23161 and 23165 instead in the range 23140-23168 which Stratford applied. This boiler type was extinct when 23144 and 23159 were cut up in August 1963 at Doncaster Works, along with J20/1 class engines 64691 and 64699.

TENDERS

When the Great Eastern introduced this 4-6-0 for its major passenger work, the under-line bridges and modest turntable diameters imposed strict limitations on the capacity and length of tender which could be put with it. 4 tons of coal and 3,700 gallons of water was all that could be carried, with total wheelbase of engine and tender limited to 48ft. 3in.. It was May 1938 before G.E. lines could accept the Group Standard 4,200 gallons tender, and by then B12s had been supplanted by B17s on many jobs - so no B12 received an upgraded tender.

Until 1924, tenders were plated at the rear with the same number as the engine to which they had first been coupled. The 10in. x 6in. rectangular cast iron plates had 2.25" high figures under G.E.R. and above STRATFORD, followed by the year the tender was built. After Grouping Stratford works incurred the trouble and expense of changing the plates to show L.N.E.R. and the 7000 addition to the number. An official *Tender Census* taken in July 1952 disclosed that only one B12 tender was not still plated 85XX, and 22 cases showed no change. The exception was a tender of similar type plated 20, built in 1907 and of 3,450 gallons capacity, and it emanated from the rebuilding of the 0-10-0 tank to run as a 0-8-0 tender engine. It came in useful for replacing 8578's tender destroyed in a collision in January 1931. Another curiosity from the *Census* was that the 1928-built tenders carried 3,670 and not 3,700 gallons. Unless some un-recorded change was made after the preserved 61572's withdrawal, it will have the tender off 8568.

LIVERIES

When these 4-6-0s became LNER class B12, none carried the superb initial painting in dark blue with scarlet lining, as shown on Volume 7's dust wrapper. That was a casualty of the 1914-18 war, replaced (to the other extreme) by a nondescript unlined grey - later engines appearing new in this dreary garb. Large brass numberplates were fitted on the cab, through to No.1570, and those in blue had G E R on the tender. When changed to grey these initials were discarded, and the tender sides were plain until, starting in 1920, the engine number was put on them in 19in. yellow figures without shading. This style even continued well into LNER years, 8500, 8524, 8526 and 8528 carrying it certainly into 1926, and maybe later, though they had lost their large numberplates at repairs in 1924, when 9in. x 5in. LNER type were fitted.

The twenty engines 1541-1560 which Beardmore built in 1920/21 were delivered painted grey, but at least some had white lining, including a large rectangular panel with rounded corners on the tender. Whilst all had G E R initials when new, it is not known how many had the white lining. 1546 definitely had it, and kept it when

the initials were painted over and 19in. yellow numbers were put on. That was probably done in 1922, because it kept its large brass numberplates, which would almost surely have been changed to the smaller LNER type at the general repair from which it was ex-works on August 1st 1923. On the other hand, 1558 out from general repair on January 6th 1923 had tender retaining G E R (albeit only faintly) but no evidence of white lining. Naturally, in the first week of new ownership, it kept its large numberplates.

The first indication of livery change appeared on No.1534 which had been selected to participate in the Directors' inspection of various styles in Marylebone station on February 22nd 1923. It had been painted Great Northern green, with L. & N.E.R. above 12in. figures on the tender, and the plate on the cab was an elliptical 9in. x 5in.. On the front buffer beam 4.5". shaded figures replaced the larger ones used by the G E R, a style the Board, it happens, had decided to make standard for express passenger engines. By July 1923 full points, and the ampersand, had been discarded, and the other workshops had ceased to use them. Stratford's difficulties with painting persisted for some years into the LNER, as exemplified by engine 1516. When ex-works on May 18th 1923 from a general repair they had managed to put it into the standard green livery with lining. At its next general repair, June to November 1926, it was rebuilt with Lentz poppet valves operated by oscillating cam gear, but nothing was done to the paint except changing 1516 to 8516 on the tender, so it still had full points and ampersand with its initials until it went to works again in September 1927. It is pertinent here to include an official comment. When the LNER Board began to consider a standard livery for locomotives the Accountants of the G.N., G.C., N.E. and G.E. were asked to provide detailed costs for painting express passenger engines. The resulting February 1923 Report gave meticulous details for a G.N., G.C., and N.E. locomotive, but there was nothing for one on the G.E. The Summary pointed out that there was very little difference in the amount of material, and cost of paints

1543E was one of the twenty built by Wm. Beardmore during 1920/21. They differed from the previous batches by being fitted with an ash ejector in the smokebox and also had a Davies & Metcalfe exhaust steam injector. The Company initials do not have full points but still include the ampersand.

Whilst at Grantham shed 61565 also worked main line stopping trains to and from Peterborough (North) as here at Great Ponton, where it is climbing to Stoke tunnel.

used, but that the G.N. seemed to employ a cheaper class of labour than the other two. The omission of any G.E. costs was explained by *"they practically do not paint their engines at all"*.

Stratford's parsimony on painting continued to show even into the 1930s on the B12 class. By 1928 the works had struggled to put most of the class into standard green lined livery with 12in. figures and 7.5" LNER in shaded transfers on the tender. Then early in 1929 it was decided to move the number from tender to cab, and for tenders to show just 12in. LNER . Stratford duly implemented the number change, but until May 1930 continued tender lettering in 7.5in. although they could have used up that stock on tank engines, on which it was the standard size.

Stratford also made themselves a problem in the position for the cab numbering, by retaining the almost semi-circular brass beading, which served no useful purpose. Squeezing the 12in. figures between it and the bottom of the cab side windows provided yet one more example of the engineering dictum that "if it doesn't look right, then it can't be right". At least fifteen, 8517, 8518, 8519, 8520, 8522, 8525, 8527, 8532, 8533, 8540, 8545, 8547, 8552, 8553 and 8556, were recorded in that odd style, which 8522 acquired as late as December 1930, and only lost in 1933 at its next general repair.

When Stratford began to transfer engines of Part 1 to the North-ern Scottish Area in April 1931, they did at least send those which had Group Standard green livery. Then their maintenance devolved on Inverurie works, which had ceased painting classes which qualified for green. For whatever reason, Inverurie did not get a supply of green paint, and so from December 1935, commencing with 8502, their B12s were put into black, lined in red. However, they recognised that their most powerful passenger engines deserved some form of respect, and so they gave them double red lining on the cab side panel, and on the tender. No other LNER class was so treated.

1939-45 war conditions caused the whole class to degenerate into unlined black paint with merely N E on the tender, that applying even to the first to be withdrawn, 8534 of Part 1 in June 1945. With laudable intentions post-war, this class was to be restored to green livery, but all that Stratford managed was one Part 3, No.1565 in March 1947, and after the demise of the LNER, it went back to black as B.R. 61565, in March 1949.

Curiously, Inverurie then turned *volte face* on colour for its B12s, no less than twenty of its 25 being put into LNER green with lining. Only 1500, 1531, 1548, 1551 and 61532 were those to miss out, but the latter did get B.R.'s lined livery, to which seven of the green painted ones were changed subsequently.

Stratford also applied the B.R. red, cream, and grey lining in its

The B12 tender carried a tool box placed fore and aft on each side at the front end. Until in the mid-1940s Stratford started to remove them, though it made slow progress. 61556 still had them at least into 1955, and Inverurie left them in place on all 25 engines that it maintained. Under the cab number, very small, is RA4, indicating the wide route availability of the class.

During 1923/24, trials were made of equipment for clearing the products of combustion from the boiler tubes, to improve steam raising. 8547, along with 8518, 8519, 8535 and 8544, was fitted with what was known as the "Superior" tube cleaner, as seen on the side of the firebox. Its results were not sufficiently encouraging to justify further applications, and the equipment was removed in 1927. This photo shows clearly the copper cap to the chimney, and that vacuum brake, and tender coal guard, have not yet been fitted.

8580, the last of the class, exhibited on an open day at its builders, Beyer-Peacock & Co on 29 September 1928.

continued use of black paint and, on the tender, in turn combined it with BRITISH RAILWAYS, emblem, and crest. 61556, 61557, and 61516 are examples illustrating that variation. Eight survived long enough to get the crest, which was introduced on the B12s with 61577 in August 1957, but all had the heraldic gaffe of the lion facing the wrong way on the right hand side of the tender and all were withdrawn without getting the mandatory correction. It will be interesting to see how preserved 61572 fares if restored to its final service painting of B.R. lined black.

Note :
Engines were cut up at either Inverurie or Stratford according to where their last shopping was carried out.

B12 class did a lot of work on the London - Southend trains and many of them were out-stationed at Southend for brief periods. 8549 is shown on the vacuum-operated turntable there.

The B12s figured greatly during the LNER pre-war exhibition period and here we have an immaculate 8579 appearing at the Stratford Silver Jubilee exhibition and works open day 4 & 5th May 1935.

About a week prior to the exhibitions the LNER advertised the events using the novel method shown on the smokebox door of 8553 in 1933.

A view which not only restores memories of the B12 engines but recalls the earlier magnificence of Liverpool Street station before the recent rebuilding.

An impressive view of maximum effort by 8571 as it nears journey's end on a down Cambridge express in the 1930s.

The first engine of the class - 1500 in original condition, and although believed to be in blue painting, the photography of the time could not pick out the red lining, although it is just possible to discern the G E R lettering on the tender. Note that protection of the superheater elements is by a valve on the side of the smokebox, a damper being used prior to the fitting of twin snifters on top of the smokebox. Only Westinghouse brake is fitted, and the tender does not have either coal guard or rails.

8500

Stratford.

To traffic 12/1911.

REPAIRS:
Str. 16/8/16-7/3/17.**G.**
Str. 12/11/20-5/2/21.**G.**
Str. 6/24.**G.**
Str. 19/2-23/7/26.**G.**
Str. 3/28.**G.** *Coal guard.*
Str. 7/28.**N/C.** *Vac. brake.*
Str. 23/12/29-7/2/30.**G.**
Str. 11-12/31.**G.** *ACFI & Tab Exch.*
Cow. 4/6/32.**L.**
Inv. 6/5/33.**G.**
Inv. 30/12/33.**H.**
Inv. 26/4/35.**H.**
Inv. 1/2-21/3/36.**G.**
Inv. 28/11/36.**H.**
Inv. 19/3/38.**H.**
Inv. 9/12/38.**L.**
Inv. 15/7/39.**H.**
Inv. 5/9/40.**L.**
Inv. 2-30/11/40.**G.**
Inv. 20/1-22/2/41.**L.** *ACFI off.*
Inv. 8/8/41.**L.**
Inv. 27/2/42.**L.**
Inv. 23/4/43.**L.**
Inv. 28/8/43.**H.**
Inv. 19/2/44.**L.**

Inv. 16-30/9/44.**H.**
Inv. 27/1-10/2/45.**L.**
Inv. 3/11-29/12/45.**G.**
Inv. 23/8-11/10/47.**G.** *Rebuilt to part 4.*

BOILERS:
1500.
1504 *(ex1504)* 7/3/17.
3809 *(new)* 5/2/21.
1559 23/7/26.
1514 *(ex8541)* 3/28.
1531 *(ex8536)* 7/2/30.
3828 *(ex8511)* 12/31.
Renumbered C1779 6/5/33.
3821 *(ex8529)* 21/3/36.
C1817 *(ex8536)* 30/11/40.
3845 *(exSTR & 8289)* 29/12/45.
4468 *(new ex DON)* 11/10/47.

SHEDS:
Ipswich.
Colchester 18/5/28.
Kittybrewster 29/12/31.
Elgin 3/38.
Haymarket 12/41.
St Margarets 3/43.
Kittybrewster 28/8/43.
Keith 12/12/43.

RENUMBERED:
1500 22/6/46.

CONDEMNED:
23/6/48.

8501

Stratford.

To traffic 2/1912.

REPAIRS:
Str. 25/10/18-27/5/19.**G.**
Str. 7/4-22/6/22.**G.**
Str. 20/4-6/7/23.**G.**
Str. 5/24.**G.**
Str. 19/11/24.**L.**
Str. 6/26.**G.**
Str. 5/4-26/5/27.**H.**
Str. 31/12/27-29/2/28.**G.** *Coal guard.*
Str. 7/28.**N/C.** *Vac.brake.*
Str. 26/8-27/9/29.**H.**
Str. 6/31.**G.** *ACFI & Tab Exch.*
Inv. 11/8/34.**H.**
Inv. 9/11/35.**L.**
Inv. 7-28/11/36.**G.**
Inv. 23/3/38.**L.**
Inv. 22-29/10/38.**L.**
Inv. 30/6/39.**H.**
Inv. 19/12/39.**L.**
Inv. 24/1/40.**L.**

Inv. 11/7/40.**L.**
Inv. 1/2-3/5/41.**G.**
Inv. 30/9/41.**L.**
Inv. 25/12/41.**L.**
Inv. 21/5/42.**L.**
Inv. 24/4/43.**L.**
Inv. 15/10/43.**L.**
Inv. 11/12/43.**H.**
Inv. 27/9/44.**L.**
Inv. 3/2-10/3/45.**G.**
Inv. 22/6-17/8/46.**G.**
Inv. 14-21/6/47.**L.**
Inv. 28/5-24/6/48.**G.**
Inv. 22/8-26/9/49.**L/I.**
Inv. 14-16/3/50.**C/L.**
Inv. 7-10/8/50.**C/L.**
Inv. 23/10-3/11/50.**C/L.**
Inv. 16-18/1/51.**N/C.**
Inv. 16/7-22/8/51.**H/I.**
Inv. 11/8-9/9/52.**C/L.**
Inv. 28-29/10/52.**N/C.**
Inv. 4/5/53.*Not repaired.*

BOILERS:
1501.
1526 *(ex1526)* 27/5/19.
1502 *(ex1502)* 22/6/22.
1501 *(ex1521)* 6/7/23.
1543 *(ex1543)* 5/24.
3833 *(new)* 29/2/28.
1287 *(ex8503)* 6/31.
Renumbered C1778 11/8/34.

WORKS CODES : Cow - Cowlairs, Dar - Darlington, Don - Doncaster, Ghd - Gateshead, Gor - Gorton, Inv - Inverurie, Str - Stratford.
REPAIR CODES : **C/H** - Casual Heavy, **C/L** - Casual Light, **G** - General, **H** - Heavy, **H/I** - Heavy Intermediate, **L** - Light, **L/I** - Light Intermediate, **N/C** - Not classified.

11

C1779 (ex8500) 28/11/36.
C1776 (ex8504 & Spare) 3/5/41.
3850 (ex8529) 10/3/45.
3841 (ex8548) 17/8/46.
3849 (ex8502 & Spare) 24/6/48.
Renumbered 23109 22/8/51.

SHEDS:
Ipswich.
Kittybrewster 21/7/31.
Elgin 1/38.
Kittybrewster 4/43.
Keith 12/12/43.

RENUMBERED:
1501 14/9/46.
61501 24/6/48.

CONDEMNED:
20/5/53.

8502

Stratford.

To traffic 2/1912.

REPAIRS:
Str. 14/6-14/12/16.**G.**
Str. 10/20.**G.**
Str. 14/12/21-25/3/22.**G.**
Str. 2/2-5/5/23.**G.**
Str. 6/24.**H.**
Str. 12/25.**G.**
Str. 7/27.**G.**
Str. 1/29.**G.** Coal guard &
vac.brake.
Str. 9-11/30.**G.**
Str. 3/31.**G.** Tab.exch.
Inv. 19/5/34.**H.**
Inv. 30/11-20/12/35.**H.**
Inv. 2/10/37.**L.**

Inv. 13/9/38.**G.**
Inv. 22/2/39.**N/C.**
Inv. 22/12/39.**H.**
Inv. 18/5/40.**L.**
Inv. 9/8/41.**H.**
Inv. 21/11/41.**L.**
Inv. 4/2/42.**L.**
Inv. 31/10/42.**L.**
Inv. 17/7/43.**G.**
Inv. 23/12/43.**L.**
Inv. 26/5/44.**L.**
Inv. 25/9/44.**L.**
Inv. 26/5-6/10/45.**H.** New cyls.
Inv. 16/2-2/3/46.**L.**
Inv. 6/7-30/8/46.**G.**
Inv. 15-22/3/47.**L.**
Inv. 15/5-12/6/48.**H.**
Inv. 2/3-6/4/51.**G.**
Inv. 25-26/7/51.**N/C.**
Inv. 3/3-2/4/52.**C/L.**
Inv. 19/1-6/2/53.**L/I.**
Inv. 14-31/12/53.**L/I.**
Inv. 25-31/3/54.**N/C.**
Inv. 7/4/54.Not repaired.

BOILERS:
1502.
1509 (ex1509) 14/12/16.
1502 (ex1509) 10/20.
1530 (ex1527) 25/3/22.
1563 (ex1563) 5/5/23.
1547 (ex1534) 12/25.
1520 (ex8554) 1/29.
1548 (ex8548) 11/30.
Renumbered C1775 19/5/34.
3855 (exStr & 8546) 13/9/38.
3849 (ex8563) 17/7/43.
C1777 (ex8563) 30/8/46.
23101 (ex1560) 6/4/51.

SHEDS:
Ipswich.
Kittybrewster 8/4/31.

Elgin 20/6/31.
Kittybrewster 3/38.
Eastfield 28/11/42.
Kittybrewster 6/43.
Keith 12/12/43.

RENUMBERED:
1502 30/8/46.
61502 12/6/48.

CONDEMNED:
30/4/54.
Never fitted with A.C.F.I.

8503

Stratford.

To traffic 3/1912.

REPAIRS:
Str. 10/10/17-26/3/18.**G.**
Str. 25/4-19/8/19.**G.**
Str. 3/22.**G.**
Str. 6/23.**G.**
Str. 9/24.**G.**
Str. 3/26.**G.**
Str. 21/1-9/2/27.**L.**
Str. 6/27.**G.**
Str. 4/28.**H.** Coal guard &
vac.brake.
Str. 14/12/29.**G.**
Str. 17/4/31.**G.** ACFI & tab exch.
Inv. 26/5/33.**H.**
Inv. 1/12/34.**H.**
Inv. 18/4/36.**H.**
Inv. 18/11/37.**G.** ACFI off.
Inv. 6/5/38.**L.**
Inv. 7/4/39.**G.**
Inv. 21/6/39.**L.**
Inv. 9/2/40.**L.**
Inv. 15/8-12/12/42.**G.**

Inv. 9/10/43.**L.**
Inv. 19/4/44.**L.**
Inv. 16/12/44.**H.**
Inv. 4-11/8/45.**L.**
Inv. 20/10-10/11/45.**H.**
Inv. 4/5-29/6/46.**G.**
Inv. 20/3-10/4/48.**G.**
Inv. 21-23/9/48.**C/L.**

BOILERS:
1503.
1513 (ex1513) 26/3/18.
3800 (new) 19/8/19.
1539 (ex1539) 3/22.
1510 (ex1511) 9/24.
1287 (new) 6/27.
1286 (ex8540) 17/4/31.
Renumbered C1776 (-) 26/5/33.
1557 (ex8526) 18/11/37.
3848 (ex Str & 8505) 7/4/39.
3842 (ex8551) 12/12/42.
1577 (ex8513) 29/6/46.
3836 (ex8511 & spare) 10/4/48.

SHEDS:
Ipswich.
Kittybrewster 20/4/31.
Elgin 20/6/31.
Eastfield 6/36.
Kittybrewster 12/36.
Haymarket 12/41.
St Margarets 3/43.
Kittybrewster 18/8/43.
Keith 12/12/43.

RENUMBERED:
1503 29/9/46.
61503 10/4/48.

CONDEMNED:
20/5/51.

1503 in original blue livery, and with G E R on the tender. I am intrigued by its carrying discs which normally indicated an express passenger train, but also a lamp on the centre iron. The only similar displays I have identified were all carried by Continental boat trains, one of them as late as 1933 by 8544 with number on cab. Since writing the above I have seen one more, which confuses the matter - see the photo of 8509 in 1933 on the 'Eastern Belle' (page 42).

From 1541's entry into service, it became standard to have a live steam injector on the left hand side. 8559 is at Stratford shed.

The Boiler was originally fed by two non-lifting injectors mounted behind the cab footsteps, and some engines still had that type into the 1930s - as here on 8534 after its June 1929 repair.

By 1946 removal of exhaust steam injectors had begun, a new live steam type being fitted instead.

The ten engines 1561-1570 which Stratford built in April to June 1920 were similar to those built by Beardmore, but this 1925 view in the station at York shows the addition of vacuum brake, made at the March 1924 repair. 1561E was allocated to Doncaster shed from February to October 1925, and is working the triangular turn, passenger train to York, then on to Hull via Market Weighton, and back to Doncaster on an express fish train.

8572 illustrates the ten engines built in 1928 by Beyer, Peacock on which there were significant detail changes. Following trials started in December 1926 on 8516, they had Lentz poppet valves driven by oscillating cam gear, with operating rod clearly visible. Although such engines were first classed B12 LNE, that was changed to Part 2 from December 1929. As built, they had pop safety valves, vacuum brake, and coal guard on tender, but were not fitted with the decorative valance to the coupled wheels, and the buffers were Group Standard type which had a square instead of circular flange. Whilst in Part 2 none were fitted with feed water heating apparatus.

8504

Stratford.

To traffic 5/1912.

REPAIRS:
Str. 18/8-26/10/16.**G.**
Str. 27/6-9/12/19.**G.**
Str. 6/23.**G.**
Str. 9/24.**G.**
Str. 5/26.**G.**
Str. 2/28.**G.** *Coal guard.*
Str. 8/28.**N/C.** *Vac.brake.*
Str. 1-4/31.**G.** *ACFI on.*
Inv. 12/8/33.**H.**
Inv. 15/9-6/10/34.**H.**
Inv. 15/8-24/9/35.**G.**
Inv. 15/5-12/6/37.**H.**
Inv. 17/12/38-25/2/39.**G.**
Inv. 12/8/39.**G.**
Inv. 6/6/40.**L.**
Inv. 4/7-8/8/42. **H.** *ACFI off.*
Inv. 13/11-18/12/43.**G.**
Inv. 30/3/44.**L.**
Inv. 19/9/44.**L.**
Inv. 17/2-31/3/45.**G.** *Reb to part 4.*
Inv. 6-13/10/45.**C/L.**
Inv. 25/5-6/7/46.**H.**
Inv. 3-5/7/47.**N/C.**
Inv. 29/3-8/5/48.**H.**

BOILERS:
1504.
1505 *(ex1505)* 26/10/16.

1532 *(ex1532)* 9/12/19.
1506 *(ex1523)* 6/23.
1533 *(ex1531)* 9/24.
3828 *(new)* 2/28.
3857 *(new)* 4/31.
Renumbered C1777 12/8/33.
C1776 *(ex8524)* 25/2/39.
1288 *(exStr)* 12/8/39.
3821 *(ex8548)* 18/12/43.
9424 *(new)* 31/3/45.

SHEDS:
Cambridge.
Norwich 28/4/30.
Cambridge 29/5/30.
Stratford 11/2/31.
Kittybrewster 13/6/31.
Eastfield 28/6/31.
Kittybrewster 5/7/31.
Eastfield 14/12/40.
St Margarets 18/8/43.
Kittybrewster 9/43.
Keith 12/12/43.
Kittybrewster 1/4/45.

RENUMBERED:
1504 20/10/46.
61504 8/5/48.

CONDEMNED:
16/6/50.

8505

Stratford.

To traffic 12/1912.

REPAIRS:
Str. 15/3-9/8/16.**G.**
Str. 17/8-2/10/17.**G.**
Str. 6/23.**G.**
Str. 3/24.**G.**
Str. 3/26.**G.**
Str. 8-10/27.**G.** *Coal guard.*
Str. 12/27.**N/C.** *ACFI on.*
Str. 14-19/5/28.**N/C.** *Vac.brake.*
Str. 11/30.**G.**
Str. 6/32.**G.**
Str. 2/34.**G.**
Str. 11/35.**G.**
Str. 14/4/37.**G.**
Str. 15/12/38.**G.**
Inv. 15/4/39.**N/C.** *Tab.exch on.*
Inv. 7/12/39.**H.**
Inv. 29/2/40.**L.**
Inv. 8/5/40.**L.**
Inv. 12/6/40.**L.**
Inv. 6/7/40.**L.**
Inv. 8/11/41.**H.**
Inv. 17-30/9/42.**N/C.**
Inv. 14/10/42.**N/C.**
Inv. 13/1/43.**L.**
Inv. 12/6/43.**L.**
Inv. 23/7/43.**H.**
Inv. 9/44-4/11/44.**G.** *Reb to part 4.*
Inv. 19/5-28/7/45.**H.**

Inv. 3-5/10/45.**N/C.**
Inv. 16/2-23/3/46.**L.**
Inv. 17/8-14/9/46.**L.**
Inv. 9-23/11/46.**L.**
Inv. 31/5-5/7/47.**H.**
Inv. 2/4/49.**G.**
Inv. 12/10/51.**C/L.**

BOILERS:
1505.
1506 *(ex spare)* 9/8/16.
1510 *(ex1510)* 2/10/17.
1507 *(ex1538)* 6/23.
1528 *(ex1508)* 3/24.
1271 *(ex8565)* 10/27.
1273 *(ex8542)* 11/30.
1579 *(ex8579)* 6/32.
1274 *(ex8530)* 2/34.
3832 *(ex8564)* 11/35.
3848 *(ex8566)* 14/4/37.
3828 *(ex8510)* 15/12/38.
9419 *(new)* 4/11/44.
4468 *(ex1500)* 2/4/49.
Renumbered 23125 12/10/51.

SHEDS:
Ipswich.
Stratford 19/12/27.
Kittybrewster 12/3/39.

RENUMBERED:
1505 21/9/46.
61505 2/4/49.

CONDEMNED:
25/3/52.

15

8516 in black livery and with the initials NE on the tender passes Stratford with a down service on 13 October 1945. Photograph H.C.Casserley

8507

Stratford.

To traffic 12/1912.

REPAIRS:
Str. 6/7-14/11/17.**G.**
Str. 20/6/19-6/2/20.**G.**
Str. 18/10/22-30/1/23.**G.**
Str. 5/24.**G.** *Vac.brake.*
Str. 12/25.**G.**
Str. 1/4-9/7/27.**G.** *Royal visit.*
Str. 3/29.**G.** *Coal guard.*
Str. 6/32.**G.** *ACFI on.*
Str. 4/34.**G.**
Str. 3/36.**G.**
Str. 13/5/38.**G.**
Str. 19/4/40.**G.**
Inv. 20/10/41.**H.**
Inv. 22/6/42.**L.**
Inv. 21/11/42.**L.**
Inv. 14/7/43.**L.**
Inv. 30/7/43.**L.**
Inv. 10/43-11/3/44.**G.** *Reb to pt 4.*
Inv. 1/8/44.**L.**
Inv. 8/9-27/10/45.**H.**
Inv. 5/1-9/2/46.**L.**
Inv. 19-26/10/46.**L.**
Inv. 5-26/7/47.**G.**
Inv. 30/10-1/11/47.**N/C.**
Inv. 17/12/48-25/1/49.**G.**
Inv. 14-25/4/50.**C/L.**
Inv. 29/9-27/10/50.**H/I.**
Inv. 23/4-9/5/51.**C/L.**
Inv. 12/10-2/11/51.**H/I.**
Inv. 19-30/5/52.**C/L.**

Inv. 9/2/53.*Not repaired*
BOILERS:
1507.
1506 *(ex1505)* 14/11/17.
1505 *(ex1504)* 6/2/20.
1273 *(ex8567)* 12/25.
3844 *(new)* 3/29.
3843 *(ex8520)* 6/32.
1576 *(ex8558)* 4/34.
3808 *(ex8561)* 3/36.
1577 *(ex8284)* 13/5/38.
3840 *(ex8285)* 19/4/40.
9411 *(new)* 11/3/44.
9410 *(ex1508)* 26/7/47.
4473 *(new)* 25/1/49.
Renumbered 23128 2/11/51.

SHEDS:
Cambridge.
Stratford 7/1/27.
Norwich 23/4/29.
Parkeston 5/6/30.
Stratford 26/3/39.
Kittybrewster 3/5/40.
Keith 26/8/51.

RENUMBERED:
1507 3/11/46.
61507 25/1/49.

CONDEMNED:
26/2/53.

8508

Stratford.

To traffic 3/1913.

REPAIRS:
Str. 12/20.**G.** *Ross pops.*
Str. 19/4-18/7/22.**G.**
Str. 3-7/24.**G.** *Vac.brake.*
Str. 10/26.**G.** *Coal guard.*
Str. 27/4-7/7/28.**G.**
Str. 9-10/31.**G.** *ACFI on.*
Str. 6/33.**G.**
Str. 7/35.**G.**
Str. 6/37.**G.**
Str. 16/6/39.**G.**
Inv. 21/6/41.**H.**
Inv. 28/1/42.**L.**
Inv. 17/7/42.**L.**
Inv. 8/10/42.**L.**
Inv. 4/1/43.**L.**
Inv. 16/7/43.**G.** *Rebuilt to part 4.*
Inv. 6/7/44.**L.**
Inv. 14/10/44.**L.**
Inv. 27/11/44.**L.**
Inv. 6/12/44.**L.**
Inv. 21/7-1/9/45.**H.**
Inv. 7/9-19/10/46.**L.**
Inv. 1-8/2/47.**N/C.**
Inv. 26/4-14/6/47.**G.**
Inv. 27-29/11/47.**N/C.**
Inv. 21/7-29/9/48.**G.**
Inv. 10-16/2/49.**C/L.**
Inv. 3/5-3/6/49.**C/L.**
Inv. 24/10-9/11/49.**C/L.**
Inv. 9/1-9/2/50.**H/I.**
Inv. 14-17/3/50.**C/L.**

Inv. 8/8-27/9/50.**C/L.**
Inv. 9/10-1/11/50.**C/L.**
Inv. 7-22/3/51.**N/C.**
Inv. 6-28/12/51.**L/I.**
Inv. 20/4/53.*Not repaired.*

BOILERS:
1508.
1536 *(ex1536)* 12/20.
1528 *(ex1517)* 18/7/22.
3824 *(new)* 7/24.
1560 *(ex8551)* 7/7/28.
1558 *(ex8555)* 10/31.
3829 *(ex8531)* 6/33.
3831 *(ex8567)* 7/35.
3856 *(ex8515)* 6/37.
3841 *(ex8288)* 16/6/39.
9410 *(new)* 16/7/43.
4467 *(new)* 14/6/47.
4470 *(new)* 29/9/48.
Renumbered *23127 28/12/51.*

SHEDS:
Parkeston.
Stratford 26/3/39.
Parkeston 3/12/39.
Stratford 17/3/44.
Kittybrewster 6/7/40.
Keith 26/5/52.

RENUMBERED:
1508 9/6/46.
61508 29/9/48.

CONDEMNED:
30/4/53.

WORKS CODES : Cow - Cowlairs, Dar - Darlington, Don - Doncaster, Ghd - Gateshead, Gor - Gorton, Inv - Inverurie, Str - Stratford.
REPAIR CODES : **C/H** - Casual Heavy, **C/L** - Casual Light, **G** - General, **H** - Heavy, **H/I** - Heavy Intermediate, **L** - Light, **L/I** - Light Intermediate, **N/C** - Not classified.

By 1931 much needed bridge strengthening enabled maximum axle weight to be lifted to 17 tons, and permitted a 5ft. larger diameter boiler to be used on the class. Its fitting was accompanied by improvements to the valve gear, and a neater arrangement of the exhaust steam injector. The opportunity was also taken to add sight screens on the cab side, change the buffers to Group Standard, and dispense with the valancing to coupled wheels. Engines were so changed from May 1932, and became Part 3, but 8559 was not reboilered until May 1936, although it had been trial engine for longer travel valves since December 1930.

Whilst still in Part 1, and before acquiring either vacuum brake or coal guard, 8509 was equipped in March 1926 with Worthington-Simpson feed water heater and pump - mounted on the left-hand side, with nothing extra on the other side. It was the only B12 so fitted, and the gear was removed in May 1929.

By 1929, Stratford seems to have abandoned all attempts to maintain the neat and tidy appearance which the class deserved. The number on cab of 8517 does not match the initials on tender either for size or alignment, and the pipework from the feed water heater just looked a shambles.

10426

In December 1927 trials began of a competitive type feed water heater, made by the French firm of Societe l'Auxiliaire des Chemins de Fer et de l'Industrie (but always referred to as just A.C.F.I.). 8523 was one of three (8505 and 8517 were the others) so fitted, and it proved sufficiently economical for fifty more sets to be ordered and fitted in 1931-33, all to engines in Part 1 of the class. No Part 2 or Part 3 ever carried A.C.F.I. and only 8502 of those remaining in Part 1 failed to receive the equipment.

8509

Stratford.

To traffic 4/1913.

REPAIRS:
Str. 10/7/16-2/3/17.**G.**
Str. 10/20.**G.**
Str. 7/24.**G.**
Str. 17/3/26.**G.** *Worthington Feed Water Heater.*
Str. 13/10/27-26/1/28.**G.** *Coal guard on tender.*
Str. 6/28.**N/C.** *Vac.brake.*
Str. 5/29.**G.** *F.W.H.removed.*
Str. 9/4-3/6/30.**G.**
Str. 2/32.**G.** *A.C.F.I.fitted.*
Str. 11/33.**G.**
Str. 25/4/35.**G.** *Rebuilt to part 3.*
Str. 5/36.**G.**
Str. 11/37.**G.**
Str. 4/39.**G.**
Str. 3/41.**G.**
Str. 2/44.**G.**
Str. 9/2-9/3/46.**G.**
Str. 8/3-5/4/47.**G.**
Str. 23-27/2/48.**L.**

BOILERS:
1509.
1502 *(ex1502)* 2/3/17.

1509 *(ex1502)* 10/20.
1521 *(ex1532)* 7/24.
3827 *(new)* 26/1/28.
3858 *(new)* 3/6/30.
3853 *(ex8515)* 11/33.
4118 *(new)* 25/4/35.
4106 *(ex8574)* 5/36.
4108 *(ex8571)* 11/37.
4124 *(ex8575)* 4/39.
4110 *(ex8574)* 3/41.
4155 *(ex8567)* 2/44.
4152 *(ex8516)* 9/3/46.
4129 *(ex1562)* 5/4/47.

SHEDS:
Norwich.
Stratford 13/3/26.
Southend 4/10/30.
Stratford 18/10/30.
Ipswich 4/11/30.
Cambridge 17/2/34.
Stratford 1/6/34.
Norwich 30/9/45.
Yarmouth 11/10/45.
Norwich 17/2/46.
Ipswich 31/5/47.

RENUMBERED:
1509 21/9/46.

CONDEMNED:
15/10/48.

8510

Stratford.

To traffic 4/1913.

REPAIRS:
Str. 4-23/4/17.**G.**
Str. 11/21.**G.**
Str. 8/2-17/5/23.**G.**
Str. 27/9/24-14/3/25.**G.**
*Str. 28/9/26-4/3/27.**G.** Coal guard on tender.*
Str. 9/5-23/7/28.**G.** *Vac.brake.*
Str. 7/1-15/3/30.**G.**
Str. 15-19/3/30.**N/C.** *Indicator gear fitted.*
Str. 4/4-9/6/31.**G.** *A.C.F.I.fitted.*
Str. 29/11/32-16/2/33.**G.**
Str. 17/5-20/7/34.**G.**
Str. 5/3-17/4/36.**G.**
Str. 12-23/10/36.**L.**
Str. 19/10-2/12/37.**G.** *Rebuilt to part 3.*
Str. 9/10-1/12/39.**G.**
Str. 4/10-22/11/41.**G.**
Str. 29/1-18/3/44.**G.**
Str. 29/3/44.**N/C.** *For ambulance train workings.*
Str. 8-17/6/44.**H.**
Str. 21/8-21/10/44.**L.**
Str. 3/1-2/2/46.**G.**

Str. 19/12/46-15/4/47.**L.**
Str. 24/8-1/9/47.**L.**
Str. 9/1-1/3/48.**G.**
Str. 22/6/49.*Not repaired.*

BOILERS:
1510.
1512 *(ex1512)* 23/4/17.
1517 *(ex1526)* 11/21.
1506 *(ex1504)* 14/3/25.
1534 *(ex8531)* 23/7/28.
3837 *(ex8564)* 15/3/30.
3821 *(ex8536)* 9/6/31.
3846 *(ex8547)* 16/2/33.
3828 *(ex8538)* 17/4/36.
4140 *(ex8567)* 2/12/37.
4102 *(ex8535)* 1/12/39.
4122 *(ex8579)* 22/11/41.
4123 *(ex8562)* 18/3/44.
4138 *(ex7488)* 17/6/44.
4117 *(ex7491)* 2/2/46.
4131 *(ex1567)* 1/3/48.

SHEDS:
Norwich.
Lowestoft 9/10/28.
Norwich 14/10/28.
Yarmouth 24/9/29.
Norwich 29/3/31.
Yarmouth 5/7/31.
Norwich 3/3/36.
Yarmouth 31/5/36.

On the production batch, the right-hand side of the engine was festooned with considerably more piping than on the trial three. Compare 8569 with 8523 and note the multiplicity of joints to be kept tight. The task for maintenance fitters was steadily reduced with the acceleration of rebuilding to Part 3, none of which were ever burdened by A.C.F.I.

The early boilers built for the Part 3 engines were fitted with four plugs on each side of the firebox for washing-out, shown on the photograph of 8559, but by 1937, new boilers were fitted with handholes for easier access. 8565 is at Ipswich, 28th March 1937.

Apart from 8502, all the engines transferred to Scotland were already fitted with A.C.F.I. when they moved, but during 1940 - 1943, Inverurie removed the equipment, as well as taking off the surplus valancing in front of the coupled wheels. 8521 is in unlined black, with the wartime reduction to the simple N E on its tender; the buffers have been changed to Group Standard buffers, and the brake pump altered to the 8in. from the usual and less powerful 6in.

Norwich 19/10/37.
Yarmouth 15/12/37.
Norwich 6/8/39.
Stratford 31/7/40.
Ipswich 19/10/45.
Stratford 2/8/46.

RENUMBERED:
1510 20/9/46.
E1510 1/3/48.

CONDEMNED:
27/6/49.

8511

Stratford.

To traffic 5/1913.

REPAIRS:
Str. 6-8/20.**G.**
Str. 1/5-7/7/23.**G.**
Str. 19/1-17/5/24.**G.**
Str. 20-30/6/24.**L.**
Str. 3/26.**G.**
Str. 6/28.**G.** *Coal guard.*
Str. 11/28.**G.**

Str. 10-11/31.**G.**
Str. 8-10/33.**G.**
Str. 10-12/35.**G.**
Str. ?/6-10/7/37.**G.**
Str. 5/39.**G.**
Str. 11/6/41.**G.** *ACFI off.*
Inv. 4/4/42.**N/C.**
Inv. 3/10/42.**L.**
Inv. 10/4/43.**H.**
Inv. 12/7/43.**L.**
Inv. 26/1/44.**L.**
Inv. 3/6/44.**L.**
Inv. 17/8/44.**L.**
Inv. 18/11/44.**H.**
Inv. 6/12/44.**L.**
Inv. 6/7-31/8/46. **G.***Reb to part 4.*
Inv. 26/4-17/5/47.**L.**
Inv. 4-6/9/47.**L.**
Inv. 25/3-15/5/48.**H.**
Inv. 8-19/11/48.**L.**
Inv. 13/4/49.**C/L.**
Inv. 5/5/50.**N/C.**

BOILERS:
1511.
1503 *(ex1519)* 8/20.
1510 *(ex1505)* 7/7/23.
1553 *(ex1553)* 17/5/24.
1552 *(ex8553)* 6/28.

3838 *(new)* 11/28.
1541 *(ex8531)* 11/31.
3854 *(ex8546)* 10/33.
3844 *(ex8520)* 12/35.
1578 *(ex8543)* 10/7/37.
3820 *(ex8570)* 5/39.
3836 *(ex8278)* 11/6/41.
4465 *(new)* 31/8/46.

SHEDS:
Parkeston.
Cambridge 7/2/29.
March 11/10/39.
Haymarket 26/2/42.
Kittybrewster 6/3/42.
Eastfield 3/45.
Kittybrewster 7/45.

RENUMBERED:
1511 31/8/46.
61511 15/5/48.

CONDEMNED:
5/5/52.

8512

Stratford.

To traffic 6/1913.

REPAIRS:
Str. 15/12/16-3/4/17.**G.**
Str. 8/3-12/9/18.**G.**
Str. 2/2-3/5/22.**G.**
Str. 30/4-20/7/23.**G.**
Str. 5/7/24-16/1/25.**G.**
Str. 19/3-11/8/26.**G.**
Str. 23/11/27-17/2/28.**G.** *Coal guard on tender.*
Str. 22/3-6/7/29.**G.**
Str. 16/5-30/6/30.**G.**
Str. 24/3-6/6/31.**G.**
Str. 22/9-15/12/32.**G.** *A.C.F.I.fitted.*
Str. 7/5-13/7/34.**G.**
Str. 12/1-26/2/36.**G.**
Str. 29/8-8/10/37.**G.** *Reb to part 3.*
Str. 30/1-31/3/39.**G.**
Str. 4/7-14/9/40.**G.** *Footsteps alt.for ambulance trains.*
Str. 8/8-3/10/42.**G.**
Str. 1/12/42-15/1/43.**H.**
Str. 22/2-5/6/43.**L.**
Str. 17/9-21/10/44.**G.**

Str. 31/10-15/12/45.**G.**
Str. 1/6-5/8/47.**G.**
Str. 2-24/11/48.**H.**
Str. 2/12/49-21/1/50.**G.**
Str. 21/6-3/8/51.**C/L.**
Str. 8/8-19/9/52.**G.**
Str. 7-24/10/53.**C/L.**
Str. 11/7-27/8/55.**G.**

BOILERS:
1512.
1500 *(ex1500)* 3/4/17.
1515 *(ex1515)* 12/9/18.
3800 *(ex1503)* 3/5/22.
1511 *(ex1515)* 16/1/25.
3850 *(new)* 6/7/29.
3849 *(ex8538)* 13/7/34.
3824 *(ex8551)* 26/2/36.
4149 *(new)* 8/10/37.
4129 *(ex8540)* 31/3/39.
4104 *(ex8553)* 14/9/40.
4144 *(ex8558)* 3/10/42.
4151 *(ex8519)* 21/10/44.
4103 *(ex8576)* 15/12/45.
4152 *(ex1509)* 5/8/47.
4130 *(ex1562)* 24/11/48.
4122 *(ex1572)* 21/1/50.
Renumbered 27926 3/8/51.
27946 *(ex1538)* 19/9/52.
27905 *(ex1578)* 27/8/55.

SHEDS:
Cambridge.
Stratford 22/5/39.
Colchester 11/11/44.
Stratford 13/12/53.

RENUMBERED:
7426 15/1/43.
1512 16/10/46.
61512 24/11/48.

CONDEMNED:
1/1/57.

In the rebuilding to Part 3, both engine and tender changed to Group Standard buffers, which Part 2 (built in 1928) had from new. They were readily identified by their square flange instead of the circular type with which Nos.1500-1570 had been fitted. Stratford, 4th August 1945. Photograph H.C.Casserley.

Difficulties soon arose on Part 2 engines through cracking of the cylinder and cam box casting, so beginning in November 1931 with No.8577, all sixteen which had been so fitted were rebuilt with piston valves, and became, or reverted to, Part 1. 8574 was only in Part 1 for sixteen months, as it was then re-boilered to Part 3.

Until 1945, Part 3 engines had exhaust steam injector on the left hand side, but those were then removed, replaced by a new type of live steam injector. Modellers could well note the toe clearance holes which have been put in the footsteps.

61538 waits in the 'excursion' platform at Grantham with a stopping service for Nottingham (Victoria) circa 1955. Photograph Rail Archive Stephenson.

8513

Stratford.

To traffic 6/1913.

REPAIRS:
Str. 14/9/17-28/2/18.**G.**
Str. 2-3/20.**G.**
Str. /22.**G.**
Str. 2-8/25.**G.**
Str. 4/27.**G.** *Coal guard.*
Str. 2/29.**G.**
Str. 4/4-4/6/30.**G.**
Str. 9-10/31.**G.** *ACFI on.*
Str. 5/33.**G.**
Str. 14-18/5/34.**L.**
Str. 2/35.**G.**
Str. 11/36.**G.**
Str. 6/38.**G.**
Str. 7/6/40.**G.**
Inv. 16/8/40.**N/C.** *Tab.exch on.*
Inv. 22/11/41.**L.**
Inv. 4/8/42.**L.**
Inv. 3-24/10/42.**H.**
Inv. 5/11/42.**N/C.**
Inv. 24/12/42.**L.**
Inv. 27/2/43.**L.**
Inv. 2/12/44.**H.**
Inv. 27/1-3/2/45.**L.**
Inv. 14-21/4/45.**L.**
Inv. 1-22/9/45.**G.**
Inv. 21/9-19/10/46.**H.**
Inv. 30/1-19/3/48.**G.**
Inv. 28/2-31/3/50.**H/I.**
Inv. 5/3-10/5/51.**N/C.**
Inv. 16-27/7/51.**C/L.**
Inv. 20/1/53.*Not repaired.*

BOILERS:

1513.
1518 *(ex1518)* 28/2/18.
1274 *(new)* 3/20.
1530 *(ex1533)* 8/25.
3855 *(new)* 4/6/30.
3837 *(ex8510)* 10/31.
3851 *(ex8545)* 5/33.
3820 *(ex8289)* 2/35.
3826 *(ex8562)* 11/36.
3837 *(ex8508)* 6/38.
1577 *(ex8507)* 7/6/40.
3858 *(ex Str & 8273)* 22/9/45.
3842 *(ex8503 & spare)* 19/3/48.

SHEDS:
Norwich.
Ipswich 10/12/27.
Colchester 27/10/31.
Stratford 26/3/39.
Kittybrewster 17/6/40.

RENUMBERED:
1513 12/8/46.
61513 19/3/48.

CONDEMNED:
18/2/53.

8514

Stratford.

To traffic 6/1913.

REPAIRS:
Str. 6/12/18-4/7/19.**G.**
Str. 11/20.**G.**
Str. 9/4-3/7/23.**G.**
Str. 17/11/24-29/5/25.**G.**

Str. 6-21/10/25.**L.**
Str. 4/2-28/5/27.**G.**
Str. 16/11/28-28/2/29. **G** *Vac.brake & coal guard..*
Str. 20/9-5/12/30.**G.**
Str. 2-12/1/31.**L.**
Str. 6/9-10/11/32.**G.** *A.C.F.I.fitted.*
Str. 10/3-18/5/34.**G.**
Str. 20/2-3/4/36.**G.**
Str. 14/10-28/11/36.**H.**
Str. 30/12/37-11/2/38.**G.** *Rb to pt3.*
Str. 24/2-5/5/39.**G.**
Str. 9/1-6/2/40.**L.**
Str. 19/4-3/7/41.**G.**
Str. 2/2-2/4/43.**G.**
Str. 26/7-21/8/43.**L.**
Str. 19/4-8/5/44.**L.**
Str. 3-30/12/44.**G.**
Str. 24/3-21/5/46.**L.**
Str. 29/12/46-20/2/47.**G.**
Str. 15/6-27/7/48.**G.**
Don. 4-14/4/49.**C/L.**
Don. 13-24/9/49.**C/H.**
Str. 11/7-19/8/50.**G.**
Str. 28/3-6/4/51.**C/L.**
Str. 4/5-14/6/52.**G.**
Str. 7-14/1/53.**C/L.**
Str. 31/1-28/2/53.**C/L.**
Str. 7/6-21/8/54.**G.**
Str. 21/10-24/11/56.**G.**
Str. 6-14/1/57.**N/C.**
Str. 18-27/11/57.**C/L.**

BOILERS:
1514.
1513 *(ex1503)* 4/7/19.
1529 *(ex1529)* 11/20.
1527 *(ex1525)* 29/5/25.
1547 *(ex8570)* 5/12/30.
1562 *(ex8532)* 10/11/32.

3847 *(ex8553)* 18/5/34.
3854 *(ex8511)* 3/4/36.
4117 *(ex8577)* 11/2/38.
4123 *(ex8550)* 5/5/39.
4163 *(new)* 3/7/41.
4158 *(ex8559)* 2/4/43.
4147 *(ex7467)* 30/12/44.
4156 *(ex8570)* 20/2/47.
4140 *(ex1537)* 27/7/48.
4120 *(ex1567)* 19/8/50.
Renumbered 27918 6/4/51.
27902 *(ex1535)* 14/6/52.
27931 *(ex1576)* 24/11/56.

SHEDS:
Cambridge.
March 15/8/41.
Cambridge 8/3/42.
Stratford 8/1/45.
Norwich 18/4/45.
Yarmouth 10/11/45.
Norwich 9/12/45.
Stratford 21/5/46.
Norwich 13/5/51.
Yarmouth 20/5/51.
Norwich 9/1/55.
Yarmouth 27/2/55.
Norwich 26/6/55.

RENUMBERED:
1514 11/10/46.
61514 24/7/48.

CONDEMNED:
7/10/59.

The original type buffers proved to be very durable, because on only four engines of Part 1 was a change to Group Standard observed - 8500, 8521, 8534 and 61528 being the ones concerned.

Due to a mishap, the gap between the withdrawal of the first and last engines of the class was no less than forty-eight years. The first engine to be taken out of traffic was 1506 which ran for only seven months before being severely damaged in a collision with a light engine at Colchester on 12 July 1913. Few photographs of 1506 exist and this view shows the engine shortly after being completed at Stratford in February 1913. For some reason the number was not reused and the replacement locomotive was allocated the number 1535.

The whole class, including those built in 1928, had wooden roof to the cab, and whilst still so fitted, had horizontal rain strips added to them. It was not until into the 1930s that the crew got the additional amenity of hinged sight screen on the cab.

8515

Stratford.

To traffic 11/1913.

REPAIRS:
Str. 4/1-25/7/18.**G.**
Str. 6-7/20.**G.**
Str. 14/3-11/4/22.**L.**
Str. 26/7/22-28/4/23.**G.**
Str. 20/6-6/12/24.**G.**
Str. 29/1-30/4/26.**G.**
Str. 16/9/27-11/1/28.**G.** *Coal guard on tender.*
Str. 1-16/11/28.**N/C.** *Vac.brake fitted.*
Str. 17/1-3/5/29.**G.**
Str. 5/6-22/8/30.**G.**
Str. 23/1-5/5/32.**G.** *A.C.F.I.fitted.*
Str. 25/5-1/8/33.**G.**
Str. 27/8-30/10/34.**G.**
Str. 7/11-31/12/35.**G.**
Str. 31/12/36-16/2/37.**G.**
Str. 5/6-28/7/38.**G.** *Reb to part 3.*
Str. 21/11-22/12/38.**L.**
Str. 21/4-12/5/39.**L.**
Str. 11/3-9/5/40.**G.** *Cab side screens fitted.*
Str. 24/12/41-21/2/42.**G.**
Str. 5/9-30/10/43.**G.**
Str. 2-23/12/44.**L.**

Str. 29/1-30/3/45.**G.**
Str. 25/10-17/11/45.**H.**
Str. 29/11/47-10/1/48.**G.**
Str. 6/2-7/3/49.**L.**
Str. 28/10-9/12/49.**G.**
Str. 20-29/6/50.**C/L.**
Str. 20/9/51. *Not repaired.*

BOILERS:
1515.
1523 *(ex1523)* 25/7/18.
1511 *(ex1511)* 7/20.
1509 *(ex1509)* 6/12/24.
1510 *(ex8503)* 11/1/28.
1537 *(ex8570)* 3/5/29.
3826 *(ex8529)* 22/8/30.
3853 *(ex8570)* 5/5/32.
1558 *(ex8508)* 1/8/33.
3856 *(ex8535)* 30/10/34.
3853 *(ex8530)* 16/2/37.
4151 *(new)* 28/7/38.
4140 *(ex8510)* 9/5/40.
4141 *(ex8530)* 21/2/42.
4113 *(ex8556)* 30/10/43.
4127 *(ex8540)* 30/3/45.
4116 *(ex8572)* 17/11/45.
4150 *(ex1577)* 10/1/48.
4111 *(ex1542)* 9/12/49.

SHEDS:
Ipswich.
Stratford 23/8/30.

Ipswich 24/9/30.
Stratford 2/8/46.
Colchester 1/7/51.

RENUMBERED:
1515 27/10/46.
61515 5/3/49.

CONDEMNED:
12/11/51.

8516

Stratford.

To traffic 11/1913.

REPAIRS:
Str. 29/1-18/5/23.**G.**
Str. 14-29/5/24.**L.**
Str. 15/6-30/11/26. **G.** *Reb to pt 2.*
Str. 27/1-18/3/27.**L.**
Str. 23/9-10/1/28.**G.** *Coal guard on tender.*
Str. 6/28.**N/C.** *Vac.brake.*
Str. 3/1-7/5/29.**G.**
Str. 8/11/30-2/3/31.**G.**
Str. 15/9-18/11/32.**G.** *Reb to pt 3.*
Str. 10/4-25/5/34.**G.**
Str. 1/10-5/12/35.**G.**
Str. 30/12/36-20/2/37.**G.**
Str. 9-29/1/38.**L.**

Str. 7/5-23/6/38.**G.**
Str. 21-31/3/39.**L.**
Str. 16/9-10/11/39.**G.**
Str. 12/8/40.**N/C.**
Str. 16/5-13/6/42.**H/I.**
Str. 15-16/9/42.**L.**
Str. 10/7-4/8/43.**L.**
Str. 8/1-19/2/44.**G.**
Str. 29/3/44.**N/C.**
Str. 19-29/4/44.**L.**
Str. 22/7-29/9/45.**G.**
Str. 18/5-14/8/47.**G.**
Str. 22/2-2/4/49.**G.**
Str. 29/7-30/8/49.**C/L.**
Str. 10/8-30/9/50.**C/L.**
Str. 28/5-4/8/51.**G.**
Str. 11-19/10/51.**C/L.**
Str. 6/8-12/9/53.**G.**
Str. 6-20/10/54.**C/L.**
Str. 23/6-13/8/55.**G.**
Str. 1-9/11/55.**N/C.**
Str. 22/3-5/4/56.**C/L.**
Str. 9/8-1/9/56.**C/L.**
Str. 11/7-4/10/57.**G.**

BOILERS:
1516.
1526 *(ex1501)* 18/5/23.
1539 *(ex8538)* 30/11/26.
3825 *(ex8548)* 7/5/29.

WORKS CODES : Cow - Cowlairs, Dar - Darlington, Don - Doncaster, Ghd - Gateshead, Gor - Gorton, Inv - Inverurie, Str - Stratford.
REPAIR CODES : **C/H** - Casual Heavy, **C/L** - Casual Light, **G** - General, **H** - Heavy, **H/I** - Heavy Intermediate, **L** - Light, **L/I** - Light Intermediate, **N/C** - Not classified.

3828 *(ex8504)* 2/3/31.
4104 *(new)* 18/11/32.
4103 *(ex8578)* 25/5/34.
4114 *(ex8578)* 5/12/35.
4119 *(ex8517)* 20/2/37.
4133 *(ex8567)* 23/6/38.
4106 *(ex8579)* 10/11/39.
4100 *(ex8578)* 13/6/42.
4152 *(ex8564)* 19/2/44.
4105 *(ex7476)* 29/9/45.
4162 *(ex8566)* 14/8/47.
4104 *(ex1550)* 2/4/49.
Renumbered 27900 - 30/9/50.
27925 *(ex1549)* 4/8/51.
27949 *(ex1537)* 12/9/53.
27903 *(ex1520)* 13/8/55.
27936 *(ex1553)* 4/10/57.

SHEDS:
Norwich.
Stratford 1/12/26.
Southend 30/11/29.
Stratford 4/1/30.
Norwich 14/10/45.
Yarmouth 21/6/46.
Ipswich 24/8/47.
Stratford 25/5/48.
Grantham 6/1/57.
Cambridge 24/3/57.
Kings Lynn 7/4/57.
Cambridge 13/10/57.

RENUMBERED:
1516 3/1/47.
61516 2/4/49.

CONDEMNED:
14/7/58.

From about 1930 there was a change to a steel cab roof, and that type had curved rain strips. The addition of a sight screen between the cab windows can also be noted.

61539, outside Keith shed in July 1949, portrays peculiarities in two respects, obvious only to the real B12 specialist. It has a shorter chimney than usual, of the type common to class J20, which used the same boiler as the B12s. Its boiler (1577) had moved from a J20 to be put on B12 class 8507 and that engine took boiler 1577 with it when transferred to Scotland in May 1940 - but it was rare for a smokebox and chimney to be included in an exchange of boilers. Is there a better answer as to how a J20 chimney managed to get to Inverurie? Then the tender repays close scrutiny, because it is actually No.2807 which the N.B. Loco.Co. built for the B17 4-6-0 of that number. When Darlington rebuilt that B17 to B2 class an ex-N.E. tender of higher capacity was coupled to it, and in June 1948 the then spare B17 tender was sent to Inverurie for further use.

At various dates between 1925 and 1931, a "Diamond" soot blower was tried on four of the class. 8567 had one from August 1925 to March 1927, the others fitted being 8521, 8528 and 8538. There was no external evidence of it, nor did it prove sufficiently worthwhile to become a standard item. Coal guard on tender was not fitted to 8567 until March 1929.

8517

Stratford.

To traffic 11/1913.

REPAIRS:
Str. 9/5-20/12/18.**G.**
Str. 22/2-12/5/22.**G.**
Str. 22-27/7/22.**L.**
Str. 4-6/23.**G.**
Str. 9/25.**G.**
Str. 10/27.**G.**
Str. 12/27.**N/C.** *ACFI on.*
Str. 7/29.**G.** *Coal guard.*
Str. 30/1/31.**G.**
Str. 7/10-30/11/32.**G.**
Str. 26/2/34.**G.** *Rebuilt to part 3.*
Str. 6/35.**G.**
Str. 12/36.**G.**
Str. 2/38.**G.**
Str. 6/39.**G.**
Str. 4/1/41.**G.**
Str. 1/43.**G.**
Str. 28/8/43.**H.**
Str. 18/11/44.**G.**
Str. 23/12/44-6/1/45.**L.**
Str. 29/9-10/11/45.**L.**
Str. 3-28/11/46.**G.**
Str. 14-26/6/47.**L.**
Str. 2/10/48.*Not repaired.*

BOILERS:
1517.
1528 (ex1528) 20/12/18.
1540 (ex1540) 12/5/22.
1274 (ex8513) 9/25.
1544 (ex8567) 7/29.

3861 (new) 30/1/31.
1547 (ex8514) 30/11/32.
4113 (new) 26/2/34.
4119 (new) 6/35.
4138 (new) 12/36.
4115 (ex8541) 2/38.
4137 (ex8573) 6/39.
4143 (ex8518) 4/1/41.
4160 (ex8568) 1/43.
4100 (ex8516) 18/11/44.
4143 (ex1540) 28/11/46.

SHEDS:
Norwich.
Stratford 19/12/27.

RENUMBERED:
1517 18/11/46.

CONDEMNED:
21/10/48.

8518

Stratford.

To traffic 12/1913.

REPAIRS:
Str. 27/7/17-10/1/18.**G.**
Str. 22/11/18-25/6/19.**G.**
Str. 20/11/23.**G.** *Superior tube cleaner.*
Str. 6/25.**G.**
Str. 11/26-1/27.**G.** *Tube cleaner off.*
Str. 9/27.**N/C.** *Vac.brake.*

Str. 7-9/28.**G.** *Coal guard on tender.*
Str. 1/32.**G.** *A.C.F.I.fitted.*
Str. 7/33.**G.**
Str. 1/2/35.**G.** *Rebuilt to part 3.*
Str. 4/36.**G.**
Str. 7/37.**G.**
Str. 2/39.**G.**
Str. 11/40.**G.**
Str. 8/42.**G.**
Str. 4/44.**G.**
Str. 19/1-16/2/46.**G.**

BOILERS:
1518.
1507 (ex1507) 10/1/18.
1537 (ex1537) 25/6/19.
1531 (ex1519) 20/11/23.
1516 (ex1523) 6/25.
1553 (ex8511) 9/28.
1573 (ex8573) 1/32.
3855 (ex8573) 7/33.
4123 (new) 1/2/35.
4121 (ex8527) 4/36.
4130 (ex8525) 7/37.
4143 (ex8561) 2/39.
4128 (ex8561) 11/40.
4115 (ex8567) 8/42.
4110 (ex8509) 4/44.
4136 (ex8567) 16/2/46.

SHEDS:
Ipswich.
Stratford 8/3/27.
Colchester 28/10/27.
Stratford 26/3/39.
Norwich 18/4/45.
Yarmouth 16/6/46.

Stratford 4/9/46.

RENUMBERED:
1518 13/6/46.

CONDEMNED:
3/12/47.

8519

Stratford.

To traffic 12/1913.

REPAIRS:
Str. 23/10/17-24/4/18.**G.**
Str. 18/7/19-18/2/20.**G.**
Str. 8/6-17/10/23.**G.**
Str. 10/7-23/10/25.**G.**
Str. 18/3-9/7/27.**G.** *'Kylala' blast pipe fitted.*
Str. 4/10/28-21/6/29.**G.** *Coal guard on tender. Rebuilt to part 2.*
Str. 16/9-28/11/30.**G.** *Steel cab roof.*
Str. 6/3-4/6/32.**G.** *A.C.F.I.fitted. Rebuilt to part 1.*
Str. 3-13/4/33.**H.**
Str. 1/12/33-8/2/34.**G.**
Str. 15/3-30/5/35.**G.** *Reb to part 3.*
Str. 10/5-3/7/36.**G.**
Str. 17/6-13/8/37.**G.**
Str. 5/2-6/4/39.**G.**
Str. 6/8-13/12/40.**G.** *Footsteps alt. for ambulance trains.*
Str. 4/4-30/5/42.**G.**
Str. 9/1-19/2/44.**G.**

On the engines sent to Scotland, straight rain strip was still to be seen on 1500 and 61504, which they kept to withdrawal.

Being at such a far outpost of the LNER, the Part 1 engines maintained at Inverurie could easily have missed out on the instruction to fit sight screens on the cab, but they were so provided. Here on the turntable at Kittybrewster's half-round shed, 8500's screen is clearly seen, and it is just possible to discern the double red lining on the black paint.

Str. 31/3-6/4/44.**N/C.**
Str. 25/5-3/6/44.**L.**
Str. 12/11-12/12/45.**G.**
Str. 8/4-19/5/47.**G.**
Str. 29/10-12/11/47.**L.**
Str. 1/4-14/5/49.**G.**
Str. 29/4-23/6/51.**G.**
Str. 10-22/9/51.**C/L.**
Str. 11/1-2/2/52.**C/L.**
Str. 20/8-3/10/53.**G.**
Str. 24/12/53-9/1/54.**C/L.**
Str. 2/11-23/12/55.**G.**
Str. 26/11/57.*Not repaired.*

BOILERS:
1519.
1503 *(ex1503)* 24/4/18.
1531 *(ex1531)* 18/2/20.
1503 *(ex1511)* 17/10/23.
1522 *(ex1520)* 23/10/25.
3826 *(new)* 9/7/27.
1552 *(ex8511)* 21/6/29.
1546 *(ex8535)* 28/11/30.
3826 *(ex8515)* 4/6/32.
1551 *(ex8569)* 8/2/34.
4117 *(new)* 30/5/35.
4135 *(new)* 3/7/36.
4121 *(ex8518)* 13/8/37.
4125 *(ex8559)* 6/4/39.
4145 *(ex8571)* 13/12/40.
4151 *(ex8564)* 30/5/42.
4125 *(ex8566)* 19/2/44.
4141 *(ex8561)* 12/12/45.
4160 *(ex1579)* 19/5/47.

4135 *(ex1565)* 14/5/49.
27922 *(ex1545)* 23/6/51.
27928 *(ex1561)* 23/12/55.

SHEDS:
Ipswich.
Stratford 25/3/25.
Norwich 9/7/27.
Stratford 29/8/27.
Ipswich 30/12/27.
Stratford 24/5/44.
Ipswich 10/10/45.
Stratford 29/7/46.
Norwich 6/1/57.

RENUMBERED:
1519 17/11/46.
61519 14/5/49.

CONDEMNED:
23/12/57.

8520

Stratford.

To traffic 4/1914.

REPAIRS:
Str. 4-6/22.**G.**
Str. 20/10/23-26/1/24.**G.**
Str. 18/4-11/8/25.**G.** *Vac.brake fitted.*

Str. 26/3-16/7/27.**G.**
Str. 24/9/28-24/1/29.**G.** *Coal guard on tender.*
Str. 20/3-28/5/30.**G.**
Str. 1/2-22/4/32.**G.**
Str. 17/6-13/7/32.**L.**
Str. 20/10-28/12/33.**G.**
Str. 24/10-12/12/35.**G.**
Str. 6/9-15/10/37.**G.**
Str. 7-10/3/38.**L.**
Str. 29/4-6/5/38.**L.**
Str. 5/12/38-6/1/39.**L.**
Str. 5/11/39-11/1/40.**G.** *Reb to pt 3.*
Str. 17/6-23/8/41.**G.**
Str. 2/4-5/6/43.**G.**
Str. 25/11-16/12/44.**G.**
Str. 28/2-1/4/46.**G.**
Str. 30/10-5/12/46.**L.**
Str. 14/10-25/11/47.**G.**
Str. 10/7-11/9/48.**H.**
Str. 22/1-15/2/49.**L.** *Tablet exch.app.fitted.*
Str. 11/6-5/8/50.**G.**
Str. 12/10-19/11/52.**G.**
Str. 2/1-26/2/55.**G.**
Str. 13/9-18/10/56.**C/L.**
Str. 5/6/57.*Not repaired.*

BOILERS:
1520.
1522 *(ex1522)* 6/22.
1538 *(ex1530)* 11/8/25.
3843 *(new)* 24/1/29.
1572 *(ex8572)* 22/4/32.

3844 *(ex8540)* 28/12/33.
1285 *(ex8553)* 12/12/35.
1565 *(ex8538)* 15/10/37.
4155 *(new)* 11/1/40.
4164 *(new)* 23/8/41.
4112 *(ex8523)* 5/6/43.
4122 *(ex8510)* 16/12/44.
4124 *(ex8569)* 1/4/46.
4137 *(ex1561)* 25/11/47.
4156 *(ex1550)* 5/8/50.
27903 *(ex1576)* 19/11/52.
27937 *(ex1564)* 26/2/55.

SHEDS:
Cambridge.
Ipswich 24/10/27.
Parkeston 3/12/27.
Cambridge 26/1/29.
Stratford 8/1/45.
Ipswich 9/10/45.
Stratford 29/7/46.
Yarmouth Beach 26/9/48.
Norwich 13/3/55.

RENUMBERED:
1520 21/7/46.
61520 11/9/48.

CONDEMNED:
24/6/57.

WORKS CODES : Cow - Cowlairs, Dar - Darlington, Don - Doncaster, Ghd - Gateshead, Gor - Gorton, Inv - Inverurie, Str - Stratford.
REPAIR CODES : **C/H** - Casual Heavy, **C/L** - Casual Light, **G** - General, **H** - Heavy, **H/I** - Heavy Intermediate, **L** - Light, **L/I** - Light Intermediate, **N/C** - Not classified.

61539 was favoured with a final general repair, to the condition seen here. It regained a chimney of normal height, and also a B12 tender, by exchange with 61513. Painting changed from LNER green to BR lined black, the appearance of which would have been improved if the larger size of emblem had been applied, which (to their credit) Stratford normally put on. Photograph Rail Archive Stephenson.

At Eastfield shed in Glasgow on June 15th 1936 (on loan, to work summer excursions on West Highland lines) 8503 is seen to be painted black, even in monochrome, when compared with the adjacent C11 class ex-North British 4-4-2. Photograph W.A.Camwell.

All the seventy engines taken over by the LNER were first fitted with Ramsbottom type safety valves; 8562 still had them in 1934.

8521

Stratford.

To traffic 4/1914.

REPAIRS:
Str. 13/12/18-4/7/19.**G.**
Str. 26/4-11/7/23.**G.**
Str. 25/2-5/25.**G.**
Str. 4/27.**G.** *Coal guard.*
Str. 12/28.**G.** *Vac.brake.*
Str. 1/30.**G.**
Str. 12/31.**G.** *ACFI on.*
Str. 12/33.**G.**
Str. 11/35.**G.**
Str. 4/37.G.
Str. 11/38.**G.**
Str. 15/2/41.**G.**
Inv. 31/7/42.**L.**
Inv. 19/10/43.**L.**
Inv. 15/9/44.**G.**
Str. 24/3-14/4/45.**L.**
Str. 8/12/45-26/1/46.**G.**
Inv. 31/8-21/9/46.**L.**
Inv. 3-30/8/47.**G.**
Inv. 27/8-1/9/48.**L.**
Inv. 21-30/9/48.**L.**
Inv. 19/2-19/3/49.**G.**
Inv. 2/2/50.**L.**
Inv. 1/12/50.**L.**

BOILERS:
1521.
1501 *(ex1501)* 4/7/19.
1502 *(ex1501)* 11/7/23.

1557 *(ex1557)* 5/25.
1536 *(ex8530)* 12/28.
1274 *(ex8517)* 1/30.
3832 *(ex8541)* 12/31.
1553 *(ex8570)* 12/33.
3852 *(ex8565)* 11/35.
1571 *(ex8568)* 4/37.
3827 *(ex8547 & spare)* 11/38.
3837 *(ex8290)* 15/2/41.
3839 *(ex8271)* 15/9/44.
3832 *(ex8293)* 26/1/46.
1288 *(ex1551)* 30/8/47.
3824 *(ex1543)* 19/3/49.

SHEDS:
Cambridge.
Stratford 19/3/39.
Haymarket 25/2/42.
St Margarets 3/43.
Kittybrewster 9/43.
Ipswich 7/6/44.
March 1/10/44.
Kittybrewster 23/6/46.

RENUMBERED:
1521 20/10/46.
61521 2/10/48.

CONDEMNED:
15/7/52.

8522

Stratford.

To traffic 4/1914.

REPAIRS:
Str. 2/22.**G.**
Str. 17/1-3/25.**G.**
Str. 10/26.**G.**
Str. 17/2-5/5/28.**G.** *Vac.brake &*
coal guard.
Str. 12/30.**G.**
Str. 3/33.**G.** *ACFI on.*
Str. 6/34.**G.**
Str. 10/35.**G.**
Str. 1/2/37. **G.** *Rebuilt to part 3.*
Str. 3/38.**G.**
Str. 6/39.**G.**
Str. 5/41.**G.**
Str. 4/43.**G.**
Str. 14/7-11/8/45.**G.**
Str. 22-25/1/47.**L.**

BOILERS:
1522.
1508 *(ex1508)* 2/22.
1549 *(ex8549)* 10/26.
3809 *(ex8549)* 5/5/28.
3830 *(ex8539)* 12/30.
3808 *(ex8281)* 3/33.
3860 *(ex8563)* 6/34.
1579 *(ex8555)* 10/35.
4141 *(new)* 1/2/37.
4111 *(ex8566)* 3/38.
4118 *(ex8566)* 6/39.

4162 *(new)* 5/41.
4128 *(ex8518)* 4/43.
4164 *(ex8545)* 11/8/45.

SHEDS:
Cambridge.
Stratford 20/2/45.

RENUMBERED:
1522 21/11/46.

CONDEMNED:
9/8/47.

8523

Stratford.

To traffic 5/1914.

REPAIRS:
Str. 7/11/17-24/5/18.**G.**
Str. 26/9/19-11/3/20.**G.**
Str. 8/2-19/6/23.**G.**
Str. 5/7-28/11/24.**G.**
Str. 11/2-11/6/26.**G.**
Str. 13/8-7/12/27.**G.** *A.C.F.I.fitted*
& coal guard on tender.
Str. 14-25/2/28.**L.**
Str. 14-25/5/28.**N/C.** *Vac.brake*
added.
Str. 25/1-12/6/29.**G.**
Str. 11/10/30-7/1/31.G.
Str. 24/4-21/7/32.**G.**
Str. 12/2-12/4/34.**G.**
Str. 23/6-5/9/35.**G.** *Reb to part 3.*

8570 of Norwich heads away from London and up the bank at Brentwood during the mid-1920s when the widening of the inner-suburban tracks from two to four lines was in progress. This engine spent its life in the far-flung outposts of the Great Eastern, allocated either at Norwich or Yarmouth for its first twenty-three years of operation; the final fourteen years were spent at Ipswich.

Str. 8/4-12/6/37.**G.**
Str. 2-8/3/38.**L.**
Str. 11-25/3/38.**L.**
Str. 26/9-2/12/38.**G.**
Str. 1/6-15/7/40.**G.**
Str. 26/9-14/11/42.**G.**
Str. 2/2-22/6/43.**L.**
Str. 29/10-2/12/44.**G.**
Str. 14/7-28/8/46.**G.**
Str. 18/3-30/4/48.**G.**
Str. 31/1-6/2/49.**L.**
Str. 7-19/3/49.**C/L.**
Str. 20/7-26/8/50.**G.**
Str. 19/12/51-26/1/52.**C/L.**
Str. 9/1-27/2/53.**G.** *After collision.*
Str. 2-10/12/53.**C/L.**
Str. 23/2/55.*Not repaired.*

BOILERS:
1523.
1519 *(ex1519)* 24/5/18.
1506 *(ex1507)* 11/3/20.
1516 *(ex1516)* 19/6/23.
1541 *(ex1541)* 28/11/24.
1540 *(ex8567)* 7/12/27.
1510 *(ex8515)* 12/6/29.
1552 *(ex8519)* 7/1/31.
1546 *(ex8519)* 21/7/32.
1542 *(ex8549)* 12/4/34.
4125 *(new)* 5/9/35.
4146 *(new)* 12/6/37.
4126 *(ex8542)* 2/12/38.
4112 *(ex8565)* 15/7/40.
4104 *(ex8512)* 14/11/42.
4144 *(ex7426)* 2/12/44.
4115 *(ex8578)* 28/8/46.

4134 *(ex1545)* 30/4/48.
4146 *(ex1571)* 26/8/50.
Renumbered 27936 26/1/52.
27916 *(ex1575)* 27/2/53.

SHEDS:
Ipswich.
Stratford 9/12/27.
Norwich 17/1/31.
Yarmouth 3/4/35.
Norwich 11/5/35.
Yarmouth 29/11/36.
Norwich 31/3/37.
Yarmouth 19/9/37.
Norwich 25/9/38.
Yarmouth 15/1/39.
Stratford 13/3/39.
Colchester 11/11/44.
Stratford 13/12/53.

RENUMBERED:
7437 14/11/42.
1523 23/8/46.
61523 24/4/48.

CONDEMNED:
21/3/55.

8524

Stratford.

To traffic 6/1914.

REPAIRS:

Str. 31/1-4/7/19.**G.**
Str. 3/23.**G.**
Str. 7/24.**G.** *Vac.brake.*
Str. 6/26.**G.**
Str. 5/28.**G.** *Coal guard.*
Str. 11/29.**G.**
Str. 6/31.**G.** *ACFI on.*
Str. 3/33.**G.**
Inv. 4/2/36.**L.**
Inv. 26/10/36.**H.**
Inv. 16/8/37.**H.**
Inv. 19/2/38.**G.**
Inv. 16/10/38.**L.**
Inv. 28/1/39.**G.**
Inv. 2/10/40.**L.**
Inv. 5/12/41.**L.**
Inv. 28/2/42.**H.**
Inv. 23/4/42.**L.**
Inv. 18/9/43.**H.**
Inv. 5/7/44.**L.**
Inv. 23/10/44.**L.**
Inv. 6/1-3/2/45.**H.**
Inv. 29/6-14/9/46.**G.** *Reb to part 4.*
Inv. 22/2-1/3/47.**L.**
Inv. 28/5-3/7/48.**G.**
Inv. 14/9-13/10/50.**G.**
Inv. 21/7-13/10/51.**L.**
Inv. 7/1-16/2/52.**H/I.**
Inv. 26/10/53.*Not repaired.*

BOILERS:
1524.
1514 *(ex1514)* 4/7/19.
1561 *(ex1561)* 7/24.
1545 *(ex8559)* 11/29.
1550 *(ex8537)* 6/31.

3833 *(ex8529)* 3/33.
Renumbered C1813 4/2/36.
C1776 *(ex8503)* 19/2/38.
C1818 *(ex8539)* 28/1/39.
4466 *(new)* 14/9/46.
9419 *(ex1505)* 13/10/50.
Renumbered 23121 13/10/51.

SHEDS:
Cambridge.
Stratford 4/1/27.
Parkeston 26/11/27.
Colchester 3/12/27.
Ipswich 14/1/28.
Stratford 20/1/28.
Ipswich 2/10/28.
Stratford 26/1/29.
Southend 26/6/30.
Norwich 14/7/30.
Yarmouth 10/10/30.
Norwich 29/3/31.
Ipswich 2/11/31.
Norwich 19/11/31.
Kittybrewster 24/4/33.
Keith 7/7/53.

RENUMBERED:
1524 14/9/46.
61524 3/7/48.

CONDEMNED:
5/11/53.

WORKS CODES : Cow - Cowlairs, Dar - Darlington, Don - Doncaster, Ghd - Gateshead, Gor - Gorton, Inv - Inverurie, Str - Stratford.
REPAIR CODES : **C/H** - Casual Heavy, **C/L** - Casual Light, **G** - General, **H** - Heavy, **H/I** - Heavy Intermediate, **L** - Light, **L/I** - Light Intermediate, **N/C** - Not classified.

Normal lubrication to the cylinders and piston valves was by a Wakefield mechanical type, mounted on the right hand frame and driven off the inside motion. 8538 also shows the change to pop safety valves, and the type and position of the whistle.

8543 demonstrates that Wakefield mechanical was not the sole type of lubricator used on the class - it had a Hulburd. The combination of one purple and one white disc above the buffer beam indicates that it had just worked, or was about to work, a freight service to Whitemoor

Until 1924 those to be numbered 8500 to 8570 were fitted only with Westinghouse type air brake for both engine and train braking, and 8559 remained so until May 1928, as here in 1927.

Inv. 29/10/43.**L.**
Inv. 14/7/44.**L.**
Inv. 17/3-28/4/45.**G.**
Inv. 8/9-6/10/45.**L.**
Inv. 19/10-16/11/46.**H.**
Inv. 17-31/5/47.**L.**
Inv. 29/11/47-10/1/48.**G.** *Rebuilt to part 4.*
Inv. 10/1-26/2/49.**H/I.**
Inv. 9/6/50.**L.**

BOILERS:
1526.
1517 *(ex1517)* 17/3/19.
1513 *(ex1514)* 7/21.
3834 *(new)* 17/3/28.
1574 *(ex8574)* 2/32.
3852 *(ex8542)* 7/33.
3826 *(ex8519)* 23/3/34.
1551 *(ex8519)* 6/35.
1557 *(ex8563)* 5/3/37.
C1778 *(ex8501)* 17/4/37.
3829 *(exStr & 8287)* 16/10/38.
1575 *(ex8563)* 21/3/42.
C1776 *(ex8501)* 28/4/45.
9411 *(ex1507)* 10/1/48.

SHEDS:
Cambridge.
Kittybrewster 30/10/26.
Cambridge 4/12/26.
March 6/1/29.
Cambridge 2/5/29.
Kittybrewster 12/3/37.
St Margarets 9/3/40.
Kittybrewster 18/8/43.

RENUMBERED:
1526 9/11/46.
61526 26/2/49.

CONDEMNED:
26/10/51.

In September 1938, at the time of the Munich crisis, precautions against possible air raids were taken very seriously indeed, especially in the London area. These tarpaulin additions to 8559 would certainly have obscured any glare from an open firebox door, but it was quickly realised that cover to such an extent was impractical for everyday conditions.

8525

Stratford.

To traffic 6/1914.

REPAIRS:
Str. 10/12/19-29/4/20.**G.**
Str. 9/4-14/7/23.**G.**
Str. 2/10/24-9/4/25.**G.**
Str. 1/10/26-18/3/27.**G.** *Vac.brake & coal guard.*
Str. 7/6-16/9/28.**G.** *Reb to part 2.*
Str. 10/8-12/10/29.**G.**
Str. 27/8-31/10/30.**G.**
Str. 8/12/31-19/3/32.**G.**
Str. 2/11/33-19/1/34.**G.** *Reb to pt 3.*
Str. 30/7-1/8/34.**L.**
Str. 30/10-14/12/34.**G.**
Str. 7/1-12/2/36.**G.**
Str. 15-28/9/36.**L.**
Str. 6/5-2/7/37.**G.**
Str. 2-16/3/38.**L.**
Str. 12/2-20/4/39.**G.**
Str. 8-23/4/40.**G.**
Str. 14/3-2/5/41.**H.**
Str. 20/7-17/10/42.**G.**
Str. 5/1-4/2/43.**L.**
Str. 13/2-29/3/44.**G.**
Str. 3-20/10/45.**G.**
Str. 2/6-24/8/47.**G.**
Str. 1/7-1/8/48.**L.**
Str. 4/6-2/7/49.**G.**

Str. 26/4-30/6/50.**H/I.**
Str. 19/4-5/5/51.**C/L.**
Str. 23/7/51.*Not repaired.*

BOILERS:
1525.
1527 *(ex1527)* 29/4/20.
1542 *(ex1542)* 9/4/25.
1549 *(ex8522)* 16/9/28.
1539 *(ex8516)* 12/10/29.
3827 *(ex8509)* 31/10/30.
3834 *(ex8526)* 19/3/32.
4111 *(new)* 19/1/34.
4130 *(new)* 12/2/36.
4116 *(ex8567)* 2/7/37.
4149 *(ex8512)* 20/4/39.
4147 *(ex8575)* 2/5/41.
4117 *(ex spare & 8573)* 17/10/42.
4118 *(ex spare & 8522)* 29/3/44.
4131 *(ex8567)* 20/10/45.
4147 *(ex1514)* 24/8/47.
4143 *(ex1517)* 2/7/49.
Renumbered 27921 5/5/51.

SHEDS:
Stratford.
Ipswich 18/3/27.
Stratford 24/5/44.
Ipswich 22/10/44.
Stratford 2/8/46.

RENUMBERED:
1525 12/1/47.

61525 2/7/49.

CONDEMNED:
6/8/51.

8526

Stratford.

To traffic 7/1914.

REPAIRS:
Str. 23/8/18-17/3/19.**G.**
Str. 2-7/21.**G.**
Str. 31/5-4/8/24.**G.**
Str. 8/26.**G.**
Str. 13/1-17/3/28.**G.**
Str. 6/28.**N/C.** *Vac.brake.*
Str. 2/32.**G.** *ACFI on.*
Str. 7/33.**G.**
Str. 7-23/3/34.**G.**
Str. 6/35.**G.**
Str. 5/3/37.**G.**
Inv. 17/4/37.**G.**
Inv. 8/6/38.**H.**
Inv. 16/10/38.**G.**
Inv. 3/7/39.**L.**
Inv. 28/10/39.**H.**
Inv. 20/7/40.**L.**
Inv. 21/3/42.**G.**
Inv. 26/9/42.**L.**
Inv. 17/7/43.**H.**

8527

Stratford.

To traffic 8/1914.

REPAIRS:
Str. 8/3-19/11/19.**G.**
Str. 9/11/21-4/3/22.**G.**
Str. 1/5-24/7/23.**G.**
Str. 5/25.**G.**
Str. 4/27.**G.** *Coal guard & vac.brake.*
Str. 9/28.**G.**
Str. 1/32.**G.** *ACFI on.*
Str. 18/1/35.**G.** *Rebuilt to part 3.*
Str. 3/36.**G.**
Str. 7/37.**G.**
Str. 3/39.**G.**
Str. 3/41.**G.**
Str. 5/43.**G.**
Str. 20/1-10/3/45.**G.**
Str. 16-30/6/45.**L.**
Str. 2-16/2/46.**L.**
Str. 4/5-1/6/46.**G.**
Str. 15-22/3/47.**L.**

WORKS CODES : Cow - Cowlairs, Dar - Darlington, Don - Doncaster, Ghd - Gateshead, Gor - Gorton, Inv - Inverurie, Str - Stratford.
REPAIR CODES : **C/H** - Casual Heavy, **C/L** - Casual Light, **G** - General, **H** - Heavy, **H/I** - Heavy Intermediate, **L** - Light, **L/I** - Light Intermediate, **N/C** - Not classified.

BOILERS:
1527.
1530 (ex1530) 19/11/19.
1512 (ex1510) 4/3/22.
1551 (ex8551) 4/27.
3803 (ex8556) 1/32.
4121 (new) 18/1/35.
4133 (new) 3/36.
4105 (ex8559) 7/37.
4101 (ex8571) 3/39.
4131 (ex8556) 3/41.
4156 (ex8533) 5/43.
4140 (ex7472) 10/3/45.
4126 (ex8559) 1/6/46.

SHEDS:
Cambridge.
Ipswich 31/10/27.
Parkeston 20/4/28.
Norwich 23/3/29.
Cambridge 25/4/29.
March 3/8/39.
Cambridge 8/3/42.
Stratford 10/3/45.

RENUMBERED:
1527 22/12/46.

CONDEMNED:
12/9/47.

8528

Stratford.

To traffic 9/1914.

REPAIRS:
Str. 1/5-9/10/18.**G.**
Str. 2/21.**G.**
Str. 10/1/25.**G.**
Str. 2/26.**G.** Soot blower on.
Str. 6/1-30/3/28.**G.** Coalguard on
& soot blower off.
Str. 3/31.**G.**
Str. 4/33.**G.** ACFI on.
Str. 5/33.**N/C.** Tab.exch.
Inv. 28/6/34.**H.**
Inv. 26/1/36.**H.**
Inv. 6/4/37.**L.**
Inv. 13/7/37.**L.**
Inv. 16/4/38.**G.**
Inv. 17/4/38.**N/C.**
Inv. 25/3/39.**H.**
Inv. 17/4/40.**L.**
Inv. 18/6/40.**L.**
Inv. 22/8/40.**L.**
Inv. 9/11/40.**L.**
Inv. 7/2/41.**L.**
Inv. 10/1/42.**L.**
Inv. 30/5/42.**G.**
Inv. 2/7/42.**L.**

Inv. 26/12/42.**G.**
Inv. 31/5/43.**L.**
Inv. 2/7/43.**L.**
Inv. 14/9/43.**L.**
Inv. 18/1/44.**L.**
Inv. 12/8/44.**H.**
Str. 6-20/1/45.**L.**
Str. 17-24/3/45.**L.**
Inv. 24/11/45-26/1/46.**H.**
Inv. 24/8-28/9/46.**L.**
Inv. 18/10-6/12/47.**G.**
Inv. 27/10-11/11/48.**L.**
Inv. 5/1-17/2/49.**G.**
Inv. 24/1-16/2/51.**L/I.**
Inv. 10/7-19/8/52.**L/I.**
Inv. 26/8-11/9/52.**N/C.**
Inv. 22/6/53.Not repaired.

BOILERS:
1528.
1500 (ex1512) 9/10/18.
1523 (ex1515) 2/21.
1563 (ex8502) 2/26.
3835 (new) 30/3/28.
1271 (ex8505) 3/31.
1550 (ex8524) 4/33.
Renumbered C1814 28/6/34.
3850 (exStr & 8532) 16/4/38.
3829 (ex8526) 30/5/42.
1574 (ex8280) 26/12/42.
3845 (ex1500) 6/12/47.

1574 (ex1528) 17/2/49.
Renumbered 23102 16/2/51.

SHEDS:
Cambridge.
March 29/3/31.
Kittybrewster 18/5/33.

RENUMBERED:
1528 11/8/46.
61528 13/11/48.

CONDEMNED:
1/7/53.

8552 in 1930 is definitely something of a hybrid with respect to its livery. Although the 12in. numbers have been compressed between the false beading and the base of the cab windows, the correct 12in. L N E R has been used on the tender. It was also an unusually late example of the steel ring on the smokebox being brightly polished although the chimney has lost its copper cap. Without any relevance to B12 class, it is interesting to draw attention to how LNER is depicted on the advertisement - *King's Cross for Scotland*. A double elliptical lozenge became very well known, but here we have it in a diamond. Maybe just as rare.

This is much more in keeping with the work on which the B12 class could be expected to be seen. In 1933 when 8509 was shedded at Cambridge, it would probably be taking this 'Eastern Belle' Pullman on its Hunstanton outing. Note that, in addition to the discs denoting an express, it also carries a lamp on the middle iron. Clearly there is much research to be done on these disc/lamp combinations.

8516 is a fair example of the 'hit and miss' attitude to doing a proper painting job to which Stratford were constrained in the 1920s. Ex-works from general repair in May 1923, Stratford had contrived to put it into the new standard green lined painting, the tender carrying L. & N. E. R. above 1516, all in shaded transfers. Its next general repair took from mid-June to end of November 1926, when it was rebuilt to Lentz poppet valves, which would inevitably make it the subject of keen attention. The engine seems to have been deprived of its lining, but the tender got nothing but a change of number from 1516 to 8516, amply justifying the Accountants' 1923 comment "that Stratford practically do not paint their engines at all".

8529

Stratford.

To traffic 10/1914.

REPAIRS:
Str. 14/2-7/7/20.**G.**
Str. 18/3-10/6/22.**G.**
Str. 24/4/24.**G.**
Str. 12/25-2/26.**G.**
Str. 7/27.**G.**
Str. 2/29.**G.** Vac.brake & coal guard.
Str. 5/30.**G.**
Str. 11/31.**G.** ACFI on.
Str. 2/33.**G.**
Str. 1/34.**G.**
Str. 12/34.**G.**
Str. 1/36.**G.**
Str. 5/37.**G.**
Str. 9/6/39.**G.** ACFI off.
Inv. 19/8/39.**N/C.** Tab.exch.
Inv. 20/3/40.**L.**
Inv. 17/1/41.**L.**
Inv. 11/12/41.**L.**
Don. 3/1-8/3/42.**L.**
Inv. 11/7/42.**G.**
Inv. 15/8/42.**L.**
Inv. 23/9/42.**L.**
Inv. 11/11/42.**L.**
Inv. 15/2/43.**L.**
Inv. 5/6/43.**H.**
Inv. 8/7/43.**L.**

Inv. 14/10/43.**L.**
Inv. 8/4/44.**L.**
Inv. 1/5/44.**L.**
Inv. 21/6/44.**L.**
Inv. 26/8-9/9/44.**G.**
Inv. 3-10/2/45.**L.**
Inv. 24/3-7/4/45.**G.**
Inv. 19-21/4/45.**N/C.**
Inv. 20/10-24/11/45.**L.**
Inv. 29/12/45-5/1/46.**L.**
Inv. 2/6-6/7/46.**L.**
Inv. 3-10/8/46.**L.**
Inv. 28/9-23/11/46.**H.**
Inv. 8-15/3/47.**L.**
Inv. 7-14/6/47.**L.**
Inv. 15-29/11/47.**L.**
Inv. 10-17/1/48.**L.**
Inv. 1-5/2/48.**L.**
Inv. 3/7-21/8/48.**G.**

BOILERS:
1529.
1519 *(ex1523)* 7/7/20.
1548 *(ex1548)* 2/26.
3826 *(ex8519)* 2/29.
3856 *(new)* 5/30.
3833 *(ex8501)* 11/31.
1272 *(ex8561)* 2/33.
3842 *(ex8537)* 1/34.
3821 *(ex8566)* 12/34.
1553 *(ex8521)* 1/36.
3852 *(ex8521)* 5/37.
1542 *(ex8532)* 9/6/39.
3850 *(ex8528)* 11/7/42.

3848 *(ex8551)* 9/9/44.
3847 *(ex8543)* 7/4/45.
3858 *(ex1513)* 21/8/48.

SHEDS:
Ipswich.
Kittybrewster 10/7/39.

RENUMBERED:
1529 11/8/46.
61529 17/4/48.

CONDEMNED:
3/2/50.

8530

Stratford.

To traffic 11/1914.

REPAIRS:
Str. 14/2-7/11/19.**G.**
Str. 6/3-20/6/23.**G.**
Str. 27/10/24-15/5/25.**G.**
Str. 17/9/26-26/2/27.**G.**
Str. 29/8-28/11/28.**G.** Vac.brake & coal guard.
Str. 12/2-11/4/30.**G.**
Str. 16/12/30-5/2/31.**L.**
Str. 27/1-15/4/32.**G.** *ACFI fitted.*
Str. 19/12/33-14/2/34.**G.**
Str. 13-28/7/34.**L.**

Str. 7/3-11/5/35.**G.** *Ch.to Rob.super.*
Str. 21/10-3/12/36.**G.**
Str. 10/3-6/5/38.**G.** *Reb to part 3.*
Str. 25/9-16/11/39.**G.**
Str. 23/3-30/5/41.**G.**
Str. 17/7-1/8/41.**L.**
Str. 14/1-6/2/42.**L.**
Str. 31/10-10/12/43.**G.**
Str. 8-10/3/44.**N/C.**
Str. 5/4/44.**N/C.** *Ambulance valve fitted.*
Str. 7/10-8/12/45.**G.**
Str. 25/1-19/3/48.**G.**
Str. 17/4-7/5/49.**C/H.**
Str. 5/2-5/5/50.**C/L.**
Str. 19/4-26/5/51.**G.**
Str. 14-16/1/52.**N/C.**
Str. 8/6-1/8/53.**C/L.**
Str. 15/3-14/5/54.**G.**
Str. 15-30/11/55.**C/L.**
Str. 24/9-2/11/56.**G.**

BOILERS:
1530.
1538 *(ex1538)* 7/11/19.
1536 *(ex1538)* 15/5/25.
3824 *(ex8508)* 28/11/28.
1554 *(ex8550)* 11/4/30.
1274 *(ex8521)* 15/4/32.
3858 *(ex8509)* 14/2/34.
3853 *(ex8509)* 11/5/35.
3837 *(ex8545)* 3/12/36.
4150 *(new)* 6/5/38.

WORKS CODES : Cow - Cowlairs, Dar - Darlington, Don - Doncaster, Ghd - Gateshead, Gor - Gorton, Inv - Inverurie, Str - Stratford.
REPAIR CODES : **C/H** - Casual Heavy, **C/L** - Casual Light, **G** - General, **H** - Heavy, **H/I** - Heavy Intermediate, **L** - Light, **L/I** - Light Intermediate, **N/C** - Not classified.

Whilst in Part 2, on January 16th 1931, the tender of 8578 was destroyed in the collision at Thorpe-le-Soken and was replaced by this tender. Numbered 20, it had been built in 1907 for converting the experimental 0-10-0 tank into a 0-8-0 tender engine, the tender becoming spare on the latter's demise. Despite being of slightly smaller water capacity, it remained coupled to 8578/61578 until December 1952.

8557, fitted in April 1927, was an early example of the remedy adopted to prevent coal spillage. Between 1926 and 1929, all had these extra coal guards added to the outer edge on both sides.

4141 (ex8567) 16/11/39.
4161 (new) 30/5/41.
4149 (ex8572) 10/12/43.
4161 (ex8549) 8/12/45.
4116 (ex1515) 19/3/48.
27919 (ex1546) 26/5/51.
27943 (ex1571) 14/5/54.
27925 (ex1540) 2/11/56.

SHEDS:
Cambridge.
Ipswich 15/12/27.
Cambridge 24/12/27.
Gorton 2/6/30.
Cambridge 9/6/30.
Stratford 23/7/40.
Colchester 2/1/43.
Stratford 16/1/43.
Yarmouth Beach 26/5/48.
Ipswich 15/10/50.
Norwich 25/2/51.
Yarmouth Beach 13/5/51.
Norwich 23/8/53.
Yarmouth Beach 30/5/54.
Norwich 25/1/59.
Cambridge 7/6/59.

RENUMBERED:
1530 23/11/46.
E1530 19/3/48.
61530 7/5/49.

CONDEMNED:
9/11/59.

8531

Stratford.

To traffic 11/1914.

REPAIRS:
Str. 16/5/19-16/1/20.**G.**
Str. 6/24.**G.**
Str. 4/26.**G.**
Str. 21/4/28.**G.** *Vac.brake & coal guard.*
Str. 5/31.**G.** *ACFI on.*
Str. 6/33.**G.** *Tab. exch. fitted.*
Inv. 14/12/34.**G.**
Inv. 11/2/36.**H.**
Inv. 27/10/36.**H.**
Inv. 22/1/38.**H.**
Inv. 11/6/38.**G.**
Inv. 14/2/39.**N/C.**
Inv. 15/7/39.**G.**
Inv. 27/7/40.**L.**
Inv. 15/10/40.**L.**
Str. 7/2/42.**H.** *ACFI removed.*
Inv. 16/10/43.**H.**
Inv. 14/4/44.**L.**
Str. 9/44.**G.**
Inv. 3/11-1/12/45.**G.**

BOILERS:
1531.
1533 (ex1533) 16/1/20.
1534 (ex1534) 6/24.
1541 (ex8523) 21/4/28.
3829 (ex8560) 5/31.
3825 (ex8541) 6/33.
Renumbered C1815 14/12/34.
C1813 (ex8524) 11/6/38.
3860 (exStr & 8276) 27/7/40.
1572 (ex8284) 1/12/45.

SHEDS:
Stratford.
Cambridge 4/1/27.
Gorton 9/6/30.
Cambridge 24/7/30.
March 14/5/31.
Kittybrewster 14/6/33.

Eastfield 2/43.
Kittybrewster 18/8/43.
Ipswich 8/6/44.
March 15/10/44.
Kittybrewster 23/6/46.

RENUMBERED:
1531 29/9/46.

CONDEMNED:
6/11/47.

8532

Stratford.

To traffic 12/1914.

REPAIRS:
Str. 13/6-4/9/19.**G.**
Str. 31/5-7/24.**G.** *Vac.brake.*
Str. 19/3-29/7/26.**G.** *Coal guard.*
Str. 6/28.**G.**
Str. 4/30.**G.** *Rebuilt to part 2.*
Str. 5/32.**G.** *Rebuilt to part 1. ACFI on.*
Str. 2/34.**G.**
Str. 11/35.**G.**
Str. 6/37.**G.**
Str. 8/4/39.**G.**
Str. 6/8/40.**L.**
Inv. 31/10/40.**L.**
Inv. 17/1/41.**L.**
Inv. 2/4/41.**L.**
Inv. 14/2/42.**H.**
Inv. 31/5/42.**L.**
Inv. 14/8/43.**H.**
Inv. 20/11/43.**L.**
Inv. 18/1/44.**L.**
Inv. 12/7/44.**L.**
Inv. 23/9/44.**L.**

Inv. 4/11/44.**L.**
Inv. 3/3-14/4/45.**H.**
Inv. 15/12/45-19/1/46.**G.**
Inv. 22/11-28/12/46.**L.**
Inv. 26/12/47-13/2/48. **G.** *R to pt 4.*
Inv. 3/2-20/5/49.**H/I.**
Inv. 26/5-6/6/49.**N/C.**
Inv. 9/8-1/9/50.**L/I.**
Inv. 26/10-14/11/51.**H/I.**
Inv. 22/6/53.*Not repaired.*

BOILERS:
1532.
1521 (ex1521) 4/9/19.
1272 (ex1568) 7/24.
3802 (ex8568) 29/7/26.
1533 (ex8504) 6/28.
1562 (ex8562) 4/30.
1554 (ex8530) 5/32.
1575 (ex8572) 2/34.
3850 (ex8535) 11/35.
1542 (ex8553) 6/37.
3826 (ex8513) 8/4/39.
C1817 (ex8500) 19/1/46.
4469 (new) 13/2/48.
Renumbered 23126 14/11/51.

SHEDS:
Parkeston.
Stratford 21/8/38.
Kittybrewster 13/8/40.
Keith 30/3/53.

RENUMBERED:
1532 11/8/46.
61532 20/5/49.

CONDEMNED:
1/7/53.

Although it never became one of the engines transferred to the Great North of Scotland, 8565 was nonetheless well travelled by Great Eastern standards, spending two years at March - having been displaced from Cambridge by the new B17 class - in 1931/2 from where it would have worked to points such as York, Doncaster and Sheffield. In 1933 it returned to the front line, working from Ipswich and Stratford until 1949 when it was sent to Grantham for duties on Lincoln and Peterborough stopping trains. From 1955 it spent its final two years of service at Peterborough, working to March and Cambridge.

The transfer of some of the class to work on the former M&GN line has also been given attention. Pictured here is 61530 calling at South Lynn on 16 August 1952. The tablet exchange apparatus for single line working is visible on the tender. Photograph L.R.Peters.

61532 was one of the four to acquire the spare B17 tenders which Darlington sent to Inverurie in June 1948. In August 1950, at Ferryhill Junction Aberdeen, it is taking the Deeside branch on its way to Ballater. Photograph C.L.Kerr.

8535 recovers from the Chorlton Junction slack and heads towards Guide Bridge with the up Liverpool - Harwich Continental boat train in 1928.

8533

Stratford.

To traffic 12/1914.

REPAIRS:
Str. 20/6-9/9/19.**G.**
Str. 12/10/22-17/2/23.**G.**
Str. 10/1-6/5/24.**G.**
Str. 12/10/25-8/1/26.**G.** *Alt.trailing axle boxes.*
Str. 19/10/27-25/2/28.**G.** *Coal guard on tender.*
Str. 24/5-6/9/29.**G.** *Reb to part 2.*
Str. 18/5-24/7/31.**G.**
Str. 24/11/32-3/2/33.**G.** *Reb to pt 1.*
Str. 16/5-10/8/34.**G.**
Str. 12/3-8/5/36.**G.**
Str. 19/9-29/10/37.**G.** *Rebuilt to part 3.*
Str. 15/3-12/5/39.**G.**
Str. 10/12/40-23/1/41.**G.**
Str. 28/2-14/3/41.**L.**
Str. 27/5-13/6/41.**L.**
Str. 27/12/41-17/1/42.**L.**
Str. 5/1-20/2/43.**G.**
Str. 6-15/4/43.**N/C.**
Str. 10/6-21/7/45.**G.**
Str. 24/1-1/3/46.**L.**
Str. 30/3-19/5/47.**G.**
Str. 8/3-14/4/48.**L.**
Str. 28/6-1/7/48.**N/C.**
Str. 4/5-11/6/49.**G.**
Str. 21-24/7/49.**N/C.**

Str. 19/8-15/9/51.**G.**
Str. 17/11-24/12/53.**G.**
Str. 7/7-5/8/55.**C/L.**
Str. 22/7-31/8/56.**G.**

BOILERS:
1533.
3801 *(new)* 9/9/19.
1507 *(ex1505)* 6/5/24.
1521 *(ex8509)* 25/2/28.
1529 *(ex8544)* 6/9/29.
1563 *(ex8538)* 24/7/31.
1580 *(ex8560)* 10/8/34.
3847 *(ex8514)* 8/5/36.
4131 *(ex8557)* 29/10/37.
4121 *(ex8519)* 12/5/39.
4156 *(new)* 23/1/41.
4133 *(ex8542)* 20/2/43.
4159 *(ex8547)* 21/7/45.
4157 *(ex1550)* 19/5/47.
4142 *(ex1535)* 11/6/49.
27928 *(ex1530)* 15/9/51.
27923 *(ex1553)* 24/12/53.
27944 *(ex1558)* 31/8/56.

SHEDS:
Stratford.
Ipswich 8/1/26.
Colchester 2/10/29.
Stratford 3/12/29.
South Lynn 22/8/48.
Ipswich 29/6/52.
South Lynn 19/10/52.
Yarmouth 5/4/53.
Ipswich 17/1/54.

Yarmouth 28/3/54.
Norwich 2/1/55.
Ipswich 7/8/55.
Yarmouth Beach 17/11/57.
Norwich 25/1/59.
Cambridge 7/6/59.

RENUMBERED:
1533 1/12/46.
61533 10/4/48.

CONDEMNED:
3/11/59.

8534

Stratford.

To traffic 12/1914.

REPAIRS:
Str. 3-20/2/23.*Painted Green.*
Str. 2/24.**G.**
Str. 11/25-23/1/26.**G.**
Str. 7/27.**G.**
Str. 7/28.**G.** *Vac.brake & coal guard.*
Str. 6/29.**G.**
Str. 6-8/32.**G.** *ACFI on.*
Str. 3/34.**G.**
Str. 6/35.**G.**
Str. 3/37.**G.**
Str. 27/4/39.**G.**
Str. 6/41.**G.**

Str. 11/43.**G.**

BOILERS:
1534.
1547 *(ex1547)* 2/24.
1525 *(ex1547)* 23/1/26.
1293 *(ex8293)* 6/29.
3827 *(ex8525)* 8/32.
1273 *(ex8554)* 3/34.
3858 *(ex8530)* 6/35.
1580 *(ex8533)* 3/37.
3858 *(ex8551)* 27/4/39.
3843 *(ex8288)* 6/41.

SHEDS:
Stratford.
Norwich 26/12/27.
Yarmouth 28/4/34.
Norwich 31/7/34.
Yarmouth 20/10/34.
Norwich 3/4/35.
Yarmouth 12/4/36.
Norwich 15/1/39.
Ipswich 13/2/44.
Yarmouth 5/11/44.

RENUMBERED:
Allocated **1534** *but not renumbered.*

CONDEMNED:
8/6/45.

8535

Stratford.

To traffic 3/1915.

REPAIRS:
Str. 6/9-7/11/23.**G.** *Superior tube cleaner.*
Str. 1/2-3/7/24.**H.** *Vac.brake added.*
Str. 22/6-9/10/25.**G.**
Str. 19/2-21/7/27.**G.** *Tube cleaner removed.*
Str. 29/11/28-9/3/29.**G.** *Coal guard on tender.*
Str. 25/4-3/7/30.**G.**
Str. 25/2-10/5/32.**G.** *ACFI fitted.*
Str. 13/6-1/8/33.**G.**
Str. 19/6-21/9/34.**G.**
Str. 23/11-14/12/34.**H.**
Str. 29/8-19/10/35.**G.** *Reb to pt 3.*
Str. 5/12/36-15/1/37.**G.**
Str. 29/9-12/10/37.**L.**
Str. 25/3-12/5/38.**G.**
Str. 9/9-9/11/39.**G.**
Str. 16/3-17/5/41.**G.**
Str. 29/11/41-9/1/42.**L.**
Str. 10-21/12/42.**L.**
Str. 27/6-1/9/43.**G.**

Str. 11/3-21/4/45.**G.**
Str. 3/1-31/3/47.**G.**
Str. 28/5-9/6/47.**L.**
Str. 18-27/11/47.**L.**
Str. 17/11-27/12/48.**G.**
Str. 14-20/5/49.**C/L.**
Str. 27/8-5/10/50.**G.**
Str. 24/7-4/8/51.**C/L.**
Str. 9-22/12/51.**C/L.**
Str. 20/4-24/5/52.**G.**
Str. 22/2-6/3/53.**N/C.**
Str. 31/1-19/3/54.**G.**
Str. 14-27/8/55.**C/L.**
Str. 22/4-2/6/56.**G.**
Str. 6/1-22/3/58.**G.**

BOILERS:
1535.
1537 *(ex1536)* 9/10/25.
1501 *(ex8542)* 21/7/27.
1546 *(ex8557)* 9/3/29.
3824 *(ex8530)* 3/7/30.
3845 *(ex8567)* 10/5/32.
3856 *(ex8571)* 1/8/33.
3850 *(ex8512)* 21/9/34.
4126 *(new)* 19/10/35.
4100 *(ex8556)* 15/1/37.
4102 *(ex8556)* 12/5/38.
4114 *(ex8576)* 9/11/39.
4124 *(ex8509)* 17/5/41.

4137 *(ex8575)* 1/9/43.
4113 *(ex8515)* 21/4/45.
4142 *(ex1565)* 31/3/47.
4153 *(ex1568)* 27/12/48.
27902 *(ex1537)* 5/10/50.
27942 *(ex1572)* 24/5/52.
27904 *(ex1542)* 2/6/56.
27917 *(ex1580)* 22/3/58.

SHEDS:
Ipswich.
Parkeston 8/7/30.
Ipswich 24/10/30.
Colchester 21/11/30.
Ipswich 23/3/31.
Stratford 11/5/46.
Ipswich 25/5/48.
Norwich 1/11/59.

RENUMBERED:
7449 21/12/42.
1535 15/6/46.
61535 24/12/48.

CONDEMNED:
11/12/59.

8536

Stratford.

To traffic 6/1915.

REPAIRS:
Str. 28/2-22/6/20.**G.**
Str. 21/10-13/11/22.**L.**
Str. 1/24.**G.**
Str. 2/5-28/7/25.**G.** *Vac.brake.*
Str. 2/27.**G.**
Str. 3/28.**G.** *Coal guard.*
Str. 2/11-21/12/29.**G.**
Str. 6/31.**G.** *ACFI on.*
Str. 3/33.**G.**
Inv. 26/1/35.**L.**
Inv. 29/2-21/3/36.**L.**
Inv. 13/6/36.**H.**
Inv. 25/2-25/3/39.**H.**
Inv. 3/6/39.**L.**
Inv. 16-30/12/39.**G.**
Inv. 3/8/40.**L.**
Inv. 4/1/41.**L.**
Inv. 28/3-6/6/42.**G.**
Inv. 28/1/43.**L.**
Inv. 29/6/43.**L.**
Inv. 13/10/43.**L.**
Inv. 5/2/44.**H.**
Inv. 30/9/44.**L.**

WORKS CODES : Cow - Cowlairs, Dar - Darlington, Don - Doncaster, Ghd - Gateshead, Gor - Gorton, Inv - Inverurie, Str - Stratford.
REPAIR CODES : **C/H** - Casual Heavy, **C/L** - Casual Light, **G** - General, **H** - Heavy, **H/I** - Heavy Intermediate, **L** - Light, **L/I** - Light Intermediate, **N/C** - Not classified.

61573 is at Purbeck Road, Cambridge, on a goods to Stratford, the date being December 4th 1958; less than a month away from its withdrawal date of January 1st 1959. From its final shopping in December 1957 it carried this B17 pattern chimney.

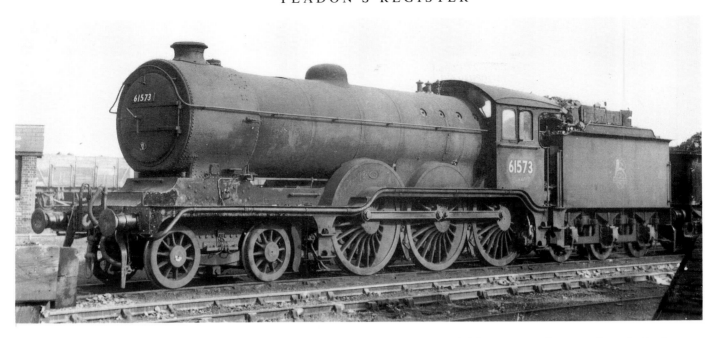

Even the standard coal guard addition did not satisfy many of the crews working B12s, especially in their latter years, and many crude wood extensions were put on unofficially to augment the insufficient four tons coal capacity. It was sad to see such capable engines deteriorate into this neglected external state.

Inv. 17/3-26/5/45.**G.**
Inv. 14-16/7/45.**N/C.**
Inv. 4-11/8/45.**L.**
Inv. 6-27/4/46.**N/C.**
Inv. 1-8/6/46.**L.**
Inv. 11/1-15/2/47.**H.**
Inv. 3-5/4/47.**L.**
Inv. 22-23/8/47.**N/C.**
Inv. 9/6-31/7/48.**G.**
Inv. 18-20/10/48.**N/C.**

Inv. 28/2-16/3/49.**L/I.**

BOILERS:
1536.
1525 *(ex1525)* 22/6/20.
1537 *(ex1518)* 1/24.
1531 *(ex1518)* 28/7/25.
3821 *(ex8287)* 21/12/29.
3801 *(ex8561)* 6/31.
3819 *(ex8290)* 3/33.

Renumbered *C1817 26/1/35.*
C1777 *(ex8504)* 30/12/39.
3854 *(ex8539)* 6/6/42.
3828 *(ex8505)* 26/5/45.

SHEDS:
Parkeston.
Ipswich 17/6/31.
Norwich 22/7/31.
Eastfield 25/4/33.

Kittybrewster 26/8/33.

RENUMBERED:
1536 31/3/46.
61536 31/7/48.

CONDEMNED:
30/12/49.

1546, one of the 1920 Beardmore batch in its original grey paint with panel of white lining on the tender. Whilst the engine's paint seems to have had some subsequent attention, the tender has simply had the G E R initials painted over so that the 19in. yellow figures could be applied.

A pleasant shot of 61552 in retirement on the G.N.o S. at Banchory on 7 July 1951. Photograph A.G.Ellis, courtesey Bruce Ellis.

8537

Stratford.

To traffic 6/1915.

REPAIRS:
Str. 8/11/18-4/7/19.**G.**
Str. 24/11/20-23/4/21.**G.**
Str. 15/9-19/12/22.**G.**
Str. 2/11/23-4/3/24.**G.**
Str. 9/10/25-19/1/26.**G.**
Str. 29/10/26-25/2/27.**G.**
Str. 28/10/27-28/1/28.**H.** *Coal guard on tender.*
Str. 16/7/28.**N/C.** *Vac.brake added.*
Str. 8/3-1/7/29.**G.**
Str. 30/10/30-28/1/31.**G.**
Str. 5-20/3/31.**L.**
Str. 2/7-13/9/32.**G.** *ACFI fitted.*
Str. 10/9-16/11/33.**G.**
Str. 7/9-31/10/34.**G.**
Str. 12/12/35-6/2/36.**G.**
Str. 2/3-22/4/37.**G.**
Str. 4-11/3/38.**L.**
Str. 1/2-28/4/39.**G.** *Reb to part 3.*
Str. 4/3-16/5/41.**G.**
Str. 13-24/4/42.**L.**
Str. 11/6-21/8/43.**G.**
Str. 14/1-1/3/45.**G.**
Str. 24/6-23/8/46.**G.**
Str. 2/5-8/6/48.**G.**
Str. 24-27/11/48.**L.** *Tablet exch.app.fitted.*
Str. 1/8-2/9/50.**G.**
Str. 10/6-1/8/53.**G.**
Str. 11/9/55-17/1/56.**G.**
Str. 25/9-12/10/56.**C/L.**

BOILERS:
1537.
1507 *(ex1518)* 4/7/19.
1524 *(ex1538)* 23/4/21.
1520 *(ex1520)* 19/12/22.
3822 *(new)* 19/1/26.
1550 *(ex8547)* 1/7/29.
3860 *(new)* 28/1/31.
3842 *(ex8554)* 13/9/32.
3845 *(ex8535)* 16/11/33.
1575 *(ex8532)* 6/2/36.
1574 *(ex8561)* 22/4/37.
4105 *(ex8527)* 28/4/39.
4103 *(ex8541)* 16/5/41.
4101 *(ex8541)* 21/8/43.
4112 *(ex8520)* 1/3/45.
4140 *(ex8527)* 23/8/46.
4164 *(ex1522)* 8/6/48.
4158 *(ex1573)* 2/9/50.
27914 *(ex1550)* 1/8/53.
27909 *(ex1569)* 17/1/56.

SHEDS:
Ipswich.
Colchester 9/10/32.
Ipswich 6/11/32.
Stratford 30/8/46.
Cambridge 6/2/49.
South Lynn 3/3/49.
Ipswich 25/7/54.

RENUMBERED:
1537 23/3/46.
61537 5/6/48.

CONDEMNED:
22/4/57.

8538

Stratford.

To traffic 6/1915.

REPAIRS:
Str. 7/3-25/7/19.**G.**
Str. 24/11/20-12/4/21.**G.**
Str. 12/5-23/8/22.**G.**
Str. 13/4-26/6/23.**G.**
Str. 5/7-13/12/24.**G.**
Str. 18/6-15/9/25.**L.**
Str. 5/7-24/11/26.**G.**
Str. 7/1-31/3/28.**G.** *Diamond soot blower. Vac.brake & coal guard.*
Str. 10/8-29/10/29.**G.**
Str. 27/1-1/4/31.**G.** *Soot blower removed.*
Str. 26/10-31/12/32.**G.** *ACFI fitted.*
Str. 23/4-5/7/34.**G.**
Str. 2/12/35-29/1/36.**G.**
Str. 11/4-10/6/37.**G.** *Reb to part 3.*
Str. 6-16/3/38.**L.**
Str. 24/3-23/4/38.**L.**
Str. 10/12/38-17/2/39.**G.**
Str. 28/7-23/10/40. **G.** *Footsteps alt.for ambulance trains.*
Str. 24/6-8/8/41.**L.**
Str. 17/4-5/5/42.**L.**
Str. 20/11/42-27/2/43.**G.**
Str. 4/3-7/4/45.**G.**
Str. 12/2-11/3/46.**L.**
Str. 2/3-23/4/47.**G.**
Str. 27/7-27/8/49.**G.**
Str. 14/1-22/3/50.**C/L.**
Str. 30/12/51-16/2/52.**G.**
Str. 23/6-14/8/54.**G.**

Str. 30/9-9/10/54.**N/C.**

BOILERS:
1538.
1524 *(ex1524)* 25/7/19.
1507 *(ex1537)* 12/4/21.
1536 *(ex1508)* 23/8/22.
1539 *(ex1503)* 13/12/24.
1526 *(ex8516)* 24/11/26.
1563 *(ex8528)* 31/3/28.
3835 *(ex8528)* 1/4/31.
3849 *(ex8563)* 31/12/32.
3828 *(ex8561)* 5/7/34.
1565 *(ex8558)* 29/1/36.
4145 *(new)* 10/6/37.
4132 *(ex8564)* 17/2/39.
4109 *(ex8544)* 23/10/40.
4120 *(ex spare & 8538)* 27/2/43.
4163 *(ex8546)* 7/4/45.
4113 *(ex1535)* 23/4/47.
4133 *(ex1569)* 27/8/49.
27935 *(ex1542)* 16/2/52.
27940 *(ex1561)* 14/8/54.

SHEDS:
Ipswich.
Gorton 31/3/28.
Ipswich 6/2/29.
Colchester 1/5/31.
Stratford 25/9/39.
Colchester 15/2/41.
Stratford 13/4/41
Grantham 29/9/49.
Peterborough 17/7/55.

RENUMBERED:
1538 25/5/46.
61538 27/8/49.

WORKS CODES : Cow - Cowlairs, Dar - Darlington, Don - Doncaster, Ghd - Gateshead, Gor - Gorton, Inv - Inverurie, Str - Stratford.
REPAIR CODES : **C/H** - Casual Heavy, **C/L** - Casual Light, **G** - General, **H** - Heavy, **H/I** - Heavy Intermediate, **L** - Light, **L/I** - Light Intermediate, **N/C** - Not classified.

CONDEMNED:
1/1/57.

8539

Stratford.

To traffic 6/1917.

REPAIRS:
Str. 2/21.**G.**
Str. 1/24.**G.**
Str. 8/25.**G.** *Vac.brake.*
Str. 2/28.**G.** *Coal guard.*
Str. 5/29.**G.**
Str. 8/30.**G.**
Str. 3/32.**G.** *ACFI on.*
Str. 4/33.**G.**
Inv. 15/2/35.**H.**
Inv. 22/2/36.**H.**
Inv. 15/9/37.**L.**
Inv. 2/2/38.**L.**
Inv. 24/12/38.**G.**
Inv. 31/5/39.**L.**
Inv. 22/10/39.**L.**
Inv. 23/2/40.**L.**
Inv. 5/4/40.**L.**
Inv. 5/6/40.**L.**
Inv. 10-31/5/41.**G.**
Inv. 21/4/42.**L.**
Inv. 22/10/42.**L.**
Inv. 13/2-6/3/43.**G.**
Inv. 8/10/43.**L.**
Inv. 11/3-1/4/44.**G.**
Inv. 24/5/44.**L.**
Inv. 16/11/44.**L.**
Inv. 13-27/1/45.**L.**
Inv. 8/9-10/11/45.**G.**
Inv. 21/12/45.**L.**
Inv. 8-22/2/47.**L.**
Inv. 31/7-5/9/48.**G.**

Inv. 11/5/50.**L.**
Inv. 29/9/50.**L.**
Inv. 5/12/50.**L.**
Inv. 7-25/1/52.**G.**
Inv. 29/6-17/7/53.**L/I.**
Inv. 6-23/10/53.**N/C.**
Inv. 5/1-5/2/54.**N/C.**
Inv. 25/5-16/6/54.**C/L.**

BOILERS:
1539.
1518 *(ex1513)* 2/21.
1532 *(ex1504)* 1/24.
3830 *(new)* 2/28.
1557 (ex8557) 8/30.
1577 *(ex8577)* 3/32.
1271 *(ex8528)* 4/33.
Renumbered C1818 15/2/35.
3854 *(exStr & 8514)* 24/12/38.
C1779 *(ex8501)* 31/5/41.
3824 *(ex8560)* 6/3/43.
3855 *(ex8502)* 1/4/44.
1577 *(ex1503)* 5/9/48.
23110 *(ex61563)* 25/1/52.

SHEDS:
Ipswich.
Kittybrewster 8/6/33.
Elgin 3/36.
Kittybrewster 1/38.
Keith 30/3/53.

RENUMBERED:
1539 11/8/46.
61539 5/9/48.

CONDEMNED:
10/11/54.

8540

Stratford.

To traffic 6/1917.

REPAIRS:
Str. 12/21.**G.**
Str. 15/3-23/6/23.**G.**
Str. 2/5-18/9/25.**G.**
Str. 21/10-6/11/26.**L.**
Str. 5/4-23/7/27.**G.**
Str. 25-30/6/28.**L.** *Vac.brake added.*
Str. 19/3-30/7/29.**G.** *Reb to part 2, Coal guard fitted.*
Str. 20/10/30-14/1/31.**G.**
Str. 3/4-24/6/32.**G.** *Reb to part 1.*
Str. 24/7-11/10/33.**G.**
Str. 21/8-18/10/34.**G.** *Reb to pt 3.*
Str. 11-30/1/35.**L.**
Str. 13/2-4/3/35.**G.**
Str. 27/4-18/6/36.**G.**
Str. 4/3-30/4/37.**G.**
Str. 4/12/38-22/2/39.**G.**
Str. 13/3-9/5/41.**G.**
Str. 22/6-18/7/42.**L.**
Str. 30/5-31/7/43.**G.**
Str. 20/10-6/11/43.**L.**
Str. 31/12/44-3/3/45.**G.**
Str. 29/5-15/6/45.**L.**
Str. 18/8-22/9/45.**L.**
Str. 26/9-7/11/46.**G.**
Str. 18/12/46-3/1/47.**L.**
Str. 13-24/1/47.**L.**
Str. 7/6-18/8/48.**G.**
Str. 15-19/11/48.**N/C.** *Tablet exch.app.fitted.*
Str. 17/11/49-31/3/50.**C/L.**
Str. 21/1-3/3/51.**H/I.**
Str. 20/8-17/10/53.**G.**
Str. 27-29/10/53.**N/C.**
Str. 30/12/55-25/2/56.**G.**

Str. 10/10/57.*Not repaired.*

BOILERS:
1540.
1500 *(ex1528)* 12/21.
1286 *(new)* 23/7/27.
1542 *(ex8294)* 14/1/31.
3844 *(ex8507)* 24/6/32.
1573 *(ex8518)* 11/10/33.
4102 *(ex8580)* 18/10/34.
4110 *(ex8572)* 18/6/36.
4129 *(ex8558)* 30/4/37.
4154 *(new)* 22/2/39.
4135 *(ex8546)* 9/5/41.
4127 *(ex8550)* 31/7/43.
4143 *(ex8573)* 3/3/45.
4154 *(ex7488)* 7/11/46.
4136 *(ex1518)* 18/8/48.
Renumbered 27915 3/3/51.
27925 *(ex1516)* 17/10/53.
27945 *(ex1575)* 25/2/56.

SHEDS:
Ipswich.
Norwich 10/12/27.
Yarmouth 3/4/28.
Norwich 10/7/38.
Yarmouth 11/3/39.
Norwich 19/5/40.
Yarmouth 24/11/40.
Ipswich 5/11/44.
Stratford 2/6/46.
South Lynn 6/12/48.
Norwich 11/7/54.
Yarmouth Beach 13/1/57.

RENUMBERED:
1540 11/5/46.
61540 7/8/48.

CONDEMNED:
28/10/57.

Stratford did do some painting - in June 1923 they put 1542, and 1543, into the green lined livery, and omitted the full points, but still included the ampersand in the Company's initials. Later that year, at an unrecorded date, 1543 had the E suffix added; then, ex-works August 23rd 1924, number 1543E had been changed to 8543 under L & N E R, and it was August 1926 before the ampersand was removed.

8570 shows that action was taken to make an orthodox presentation of number and initials, but the heater pipework offered little scope for improvement. It is extremely unlikely that any model-maker will desecrate a B12 with such uncouth additions, but he would need to decide on which pipework arrangement to adopt. 8517 had one of the three trial sets in which the main pipe enters the front end of the right hand cylinder, but 8570 got one of the production sets where that pipe was extended to go into the cylinder from below - and there were other differences.

61520 is an attractive example of the British Railways lined black livery with large emblem as used from 1949 to 1957, but is included to illustrate a much smaller detail. The tender has been fitted with tablet exchanging apparatus to enable it to work on the single line sections of the former M&GN, where the Whittaker type was employed. Six others, 61530, 61533, 61537, 61540, 61545 and 61568, were similarly fitted.

There were times when Stratford could match the other works for quality of painting as indicated by 8507 on Wednesday July 6th 1927, when on parade for inspection by King George V and Queen Mary during a Royal Visit to Stratford.

8541

Beardmore 135.

To traffic 6/1920.

REPAIRS:
Str. 21/2-8/6/23.**G.**
Str. 4/4-16/8/24.**G.**
Str. 11/2-24/6/26.**G.**
Str. 21/10/27-22/2/28.**G.** *Coal guard on tender.*
Str. 28/9-13/12/29.**G.**
Str. 14/2-21/4/31.**G.**
Str. 25/5-2/7/32.**H.**
Str. 6/3-12/5/33.**G.**
Str. 13/11/34-8/1/35.**G.**
Str. 26/3-23/5/36.**G.** *Reb to part 3.*
Str. 5/2-18/3/37.**L.**
Str. 5/12/37-14/1/38.**G.**
Str. 1-2/3/38.**L.**
Str. 2/11-9/12/38.**L.**
Str. 14/5-13/7/39.**G.**
Str. 18/1-15/3/41.**G.**
Str. 3-25/4/41.**H.**
Str. 6/3-28/5/43.**G.**
Str. 17/12/44-8/2/45.**G.**
Str. 31/10-17/12/45.**L.**
Str. 5/1-25/2/47.**G.**

Str. 14-22/4/47.**L.**
Str. 23/1-3/3/49.**G.**
Str. 29/3-9/4/49.**C/L.**
Str. 7/5-23/6/50.**C/L.**
Str. 5/10-9/12/50.**C/L.**
Str. 2/12/51-26/1/52.**G.**
Str. 1-20/8/52.**C/L.**
Str. 10/11/53-2/1/54.**G.**
Str. 30/11/54-29/1/55.**C/L.** *After collision.*
Str. 9-29/3/56.**C/L.**

BOILERS:
1541.
1514 *(ex1524)* 16/8/24.
3832 *(new)* 22/2/28.
3825 *(ex8516)* 21/4/31.
3859 *(ex8548)* 12/5/33.
1573 *(ex8540)* 8/1/35.
4115 *(ex8579)* 23/5/36.
4107 *(ex8573)* 14/1/38.
4103 *(ex8578)* 13/7/39.
4120 *(ex8580)* 15/3/41.
4101 *(ex8527)* 25/4/41.
4162 *(ex8522)* 28/5/43.
4139 (ex8579) 8/2/45.
4110 *(ex8518)* 25/2/47.
4155 *(ex1572)* 3/3/49.
Renumbered 27908 9/12/50.

27917 *(ex1565)* 26/1/52.
27939 (ex1568) 2/1/54.

SHEDS:
Stratford.
Ipswich 3/10/28.
Stratford 9/1/29.
Southend 24/5/30.
Stratford 31/5/30.
Southend 26/7/30.
Stratford 16/8/30.
Grantham 20/11/49.

RENUMBERED:
1541 15/6/46.
61541 26/2/49.

CONDEMNED:
1/1/57.

8542

Beardmore 136.

To traffic 6/1920.

REPAIRS:
Str. 26/2-29/6/23.**G.**

Str. 3/9-20/12/24.**G.**
Str. 15/4-17/9/26.**G.** *Coal guard on tender.*
Str. 30/3-13/4/27.**H.**
Str. 2/1-20/4/29.**G.**
Str. 3/4-10/6/30.**G.**
Str. 5/11/31-26/2/32.**G.** *ACFI fitted.*
Str. 20/4-29/6/33.**G.**
Str. 27/11/34-1/2/35.**G.** *Reb to pt 3.*
Str. 30/1-13/3/36.**G.**
Str. 31/3-26/5/37.**G.**
Str. 7-26/11/37.**L.**
Str. 21/9-15/11/38.**G.**
Str. 12/2-19/4/40.**G.**
Str. 15-16/5/40.**L.**
Str. 27/12/41-14/2/42.**G.**
Str. 20/5-12/6/42.**L.**
Str. 16-18/9/42.**L.**
Str. 14/11-18/12/43.**G.**
Str. 20-21/3/44.**N/C.**
Str. 18-19/4/44.**N/C.** *Ambulance valve fitted.*
Str. 8-10/6/44.**L.**
Str. 30/9-3/11/45.**G.**
Str. 20/8-28/10/47.**G.**
Str. 15/7-27/8/49.**G.**
Str. 5-22/9/49.**N/C.**
Str. 20/11/51-5/1/52.**G.**
Str. 17/9-31/10/53.**G.**

WORKS CODES : Cow - Cowlairs, Dar - Darlington, Don - Doncaster, Ghd - Gateshead, Gor - Gorton, Inv - Inverurie, Str - Stratford.
REPAIR CODES : **C/H** - Casual Heavy, **C/L** - Casual Light, **G** - General, **H** - Heavy, **H/I** - Heavy Intermediate, **L** - Light, **L/I** - Light Intermediate, **N/C** - Not classified.

Str. 4/2-29/3/56.**G.**

BOILERS:
1542.
1501 *(ex1501)* 20/12/24.
1564 *(ex8564)* 13/4/27.
1273 *(ex8507)* 20/4/29.
3852 *(new)* 10/6/30.
1543 *(ex8566)* 29/6/33.
4122 *(new)* 1/2/35.
4120 *(ex8557)* 13/3/36.
4126 *(ex8535)* 26/5/37.
4144 *(ex8553)* 15/11/38.
4133 *(ex8516)* 19/4/40.
4102 *(ex8510)* 14/2/42.
4148 *(ex8576)* 18/12/43.
4121 *(ex8554)* 3/11/45.
4111 *(ex1549)* 28/10/47.
4101 *(ex1578)* 27/8/49.
27933 *(ex1579)* 5/1/52.
27904 *(ex1569)* 31/10/53.
27933 *(ex1572)* 29/3/56.

SHEDS:
Stratford.
Norwich 11/12/26.
Yarmouth 29/3/31.
Norwich 5/7/31.
Stratford 29/6/33.
Norwich 13/5/51.
Yarmouth 17/6/51.
Norwich 9/1/55.

RENUMBERED:
1542 21/9/46.
61542 27/8/49.

CONDEMNED:
14/7/58.

8543

Beardmore 137.

To traffic 7/1920.

REPAIRS:
Str. 16/8/23.**G.**
Str. 30/4-23/8/24.**G.**
Str. 8/26.**G.**
Str. 5/1-3/3/28.**G.**
Str. 5-12/5/28.**N/C.** *vac brake & coal guard.*
Str. 11/30.**G.**
Str. 7/32.**G.** *ACFI on.*
Str. 2/34.**G.**
Str. 11/35.**G.**
Str. 4/37.**G.**
Str. 23/10-16/12/37.**L.**
Str. 20/12/38.**H.**
Inv. 14/2/39.**N/C.** *Tab.exch.*
Inv. 23/2/40.**L.**
Inv. 4-25/5/40.**H.**
Inv. 15/7/42.**L.**
Inv. 6/2/43.**H.**
Inv. 2-23/9/44.**G.**
Inv. 20-27/1/45.**N/C.**
Inv. 17/2-3/3/45.**L.**
Inv. 21/4-5/5/45.**L.**
Inv. 30/6-14/7/45.**H.**
Inv. 5/1-2/2/46.**L.**
Inv. 15-22/6/46.**L.**
Inv. 30/11/46-18/1/47.**H.**
Inv. 7-21/2/48.**L.**
Inv. 29/4-3/11/48.**G.**
Inv. 22/6-7/7/50.**L/I.**
Inv. 15/11-7/12/51.**H/I.**
Inv. 24/3-4/4/52.**C/L.**
Inv. 21-23/5/52.**C/L.**
Inv. 30/3-10/4/53.**N/C.**

BOILERS:
1543.
3801 *(ex1533)* 23/8/24.
3831 *(new)* 3/3/28.
3820 *(ex8274)* 11/30.
1285 *(ex8271)* 7/32.

1557 *(ex8575)* 2/34.
1578 *(ex8552)* 11/35.
1575 *(ex8537)* 4/37.
3847 *(ex8533)* 20/12/38.
3824 *(ex8539)* 23/9/44.
3829 *(ex1552)* 3/11/48.
Renumbered 23104 7/12/51.

SHEDS:
Stratford.
Southend 31/5/30.
Stratford 28/6/30.
Southend 20/9/30.
Stratford 27/9/30.
Kittybrewster 19/1/39.
Eastfield 7/12/40.
Kittybrewster 18/8/43.

RENUMBERED:
1543 11/5/46.
61543 3/11/48.

CONDEMNED:
19/6/53.

8544

Beardmore 138.

To traffic 8/1920.

REPAIRS:
Str. 12/2/24.**G.** *Superior tube cleaner.*
Str. 7/25.**G.** *Vac.brake.*
Str. 7/27.**G.** *Tube cleaner off.*
Str. 5/29.**G.** *Coal guard.*
Str. 7/32.**G.** *ACFI on.*
Str. 12/33.**G.**
Str. 12/2/35.**G.** *Rebuilt to part 3.*
Str. 1/36.**G.**
Str. 4/37.**G.**
Str. 1/3/38.**L.**

Str. 11/38.**G.**
Str. 9/40.**G.**
Str. 5/42.**G.**
Str. 6/43.**G.**
Str. 11/44.**G.**
Str. 5-26/1/46.**G.**
Str. 12-26/10/46.**L.**

BOILERS:
1544.
1518 *(ex1539)* 12/2/24.
1529 *(ex1514)* 7/25.
3800 *(ex8546)* 5/29.
3824 *(ex8535)* 7/32.
1549 *(ex8556)* 12/33.
4124 *(new)* 12/2/35.
4103 *(ex8516)* 1/36.
4127 *(ex8555)* 4/37.
4109 *(ex8555)* 11/38.
4153 *(ex8564)* 9/40.
4105 *(ex8537)* 5/42.
4130 *(ex8577)* 6/43.
4153 *(ex8561)* 11/44.
4118 *(ex8525)* 26/1/46.

SHEDS:
Stratford.
Southend 4/1/30.
Stratford 18/1/30.
Ipswich 7/7/32.
Colchester 23/11/44.
Stratford 25/1/47.

RENUMBERED:
1544 10/9/46.

CONDEMNED:
26/9/47.

61501 at Kttybrewster in late 1948 wearing lined green livery with BRITISH RAILWAYS in full.

1545 pauses at Gorleston-on-Sea on 17 May 1948 with the 15.25 Yarmouth (Beach) - Lowestoft (Central). Photograph W.A.Camwell.

1565 was the only B12 to which Stratford restored the green lined painting - demonstrated here ex-works, April 1st 1947. Shaded transfers were not available for it, and due to a mistake in Doncaster drawing office, the figures 6 and 9 issued were not true Gill Sans.

8545

Beardmore 139.

To traffic 9/1920.

REPAIRS:
Str. 10/10/23-22/3/24.**G.**
Str. 13/10/25-19/3/26.**G.**
Str. 30/3-29/4/27.**L.**
Str. 20/10/27-4/2/28.**G.** *Coal guard on tender & vacuum brake.*
Str. 4/2-12/7/29.**G.**
Str. 13/12/30-25/2/31.**G.**
Str. 3/10-14/11/31.**G.**
Str. 24/1-24/3/33.**G.**
Str. 1/10/34-16/3/35.**G.**
Str. 26/11-5/12/35.**L.**
Str. 15/9-6/11/36.**G.** *Reb to part 3.*
Str. 20/12/36-26/1/37.**L.**
Str. 20/5-4/6/37.**L.**
Str. 3/3-14/4/38.**G.**
Str. 18/9-17/11/39.**G.**
Str. 19-28/2/41.**L.**
Str. 21/3-23/5/41.**G.**
Str. 9/5-17/7/43.**G.**
Str. 28/10-26/11/43.**L.**
Str. 25/3-28/4/45.**G.**
Str. 18/5/46-1/1/47.**L.**
Str. 7/12/47-17/1/48.**G.**
Str. 17-18/2/48.**N/C.**
Str. 20/8-29/9/50.**G.**
Str. 27/1-15/2/52.**C/L.**
Str. 9/9-18/10/52.**G.**
Str. 26/4-21/5/54.**C/L.**

Str. 29/10-4/12/54.**G.**
Str. 10-22/11/55.**C/L.**

BOILERS:
1545.
1519 *(ex1529)* 19/3/26.
3851 *(new)* 12/7/29.
3848 *(ex8559)* 24/3/33.
3837 *(ex8546)* 16/3/35.
4136 *(new)* 6/11/36.
4138 *(ex8517)* 14/4/38.
4142 *(ex8572)* 17/11/39.
4159 *(new)* 23/5/41.
4164 *(ex8520)* 17/7/43.
4134 *(ex8566)* 28/4/45.
4159 *(ex1533)* 17/1/48.
27901 *(ex1575)* 29/9/50.
27947 *(ex1545)* 18/10/52.
27921 *(ex1565)* 4/12/54.

SHEDS:
Stratford.
Southend 19/7/30.
Stratford 2/8/30.
Southend 25/10/30.
Stratford 15/11/30.
Colchester 20/10/45.
Stratford 7/12/46.
Yarmouth Beach 27/4/48.
Norwich 15/10/50.
Yarmouth 7/1/51.
Yarmouth Beach 17/6/51.
Yarmouth 27/6/54.
Norwich 12/9/54.
Yarmouth Beach 2/1/55.

RENUMBERED:
1545 2/10/46.
61545 29/9/50.

CONDEMNED:
1/1/57.

8546

Beardmore 140.

To traffic 9/1920.

REPAIRS:
Str. 18/4-1/8/23.**G.**
Str. 25/9/24-11/3/25.**G.**
Str. 28/10/26-25/3/27.**G.** *Vac.brake Coal guard on tender.*
Str. 26/10/28-21/2/29.**G.**
Str. 14/2-25/4/30.**G.**
Str. 21/11/31-6/2/32.**G.** *ACFI fitted.*
Str. 18/4-16/6/33.**G.**
Str. 20/11/34-12/1/35.**G.**
Str. 19/4-11/6/36.**G.** *ACFI RH side fitted with exhaust injector.*
Str. 18/12/37-4/2/38.**G.** *Reb to pt 3.*
Str. 1/5-29/6/39.**G.**
Str. 13/1-7/3/41.**G.**
Str. 23/3-21/5/43.**G.**
Str. 21/1-16/3/45.**G.**
Str. 8/7-8/9/45.**L.**
Str. 23/11-5/12/45.**L.**

Str. 17/1-14/2/46.**L.**
Str. 21/2-9/3/46.**L.**
Str. 16/3-23/4/47.**G.**
Str. 2-19/6/48.**L.**
Str. 28/1-30/3/49.**G.** *Cont.blow down fitted.*
Str. 23/11-28/12/50.**G.**
Str. 19-28/6/52.**C/L.**
Str. 29/10-6/12/52.**G.**
Str. 3-19/9/53.**C/L.**
Str. 27/10-11/12/54.**G.**
Str. 14/12/55-18/1/56.**C/L.**
Str. 22/3-14/4/56.**N/C.**
Str. 29/11/56-5/1/57.**G.**
Str. 7/5/59.*Not repaired.*

BOILERS:
1546.
3800 *(ex1512)* 11/3/25.
1538 *(ex8520)* 21/2/29.
3854 *(new)* 25/4/30.
3837 *(ex8513)* 16/6/33.
3842 *(ex8529)* 12/1/35.
3855 *(ex8550)* 11/6/36.
4134 *(ex8579)* 4/2/38.
4135 *(ex8556)* 29/6/39.
4116 *(ex8566)* 7/3/41.
4163 *(ex8514)* 21/5/43.
4158 *(ex8514)* 16/3/45.
4139 *(ex1541)* 23/4/47.
4106 *(ex1554)* 30/3/49.
27909 *(ex1523)* 28/12/50.
27911 *(ex1549)* 6/12/52.
27907 *(ex1580)* 11/12/54.
27927 *(ex1570)* 5/1/57.

WORKS CODES : Cow - Cowlairs, Dar - Darlington, Don - Doncaster, Ghd - Gateshead, Gor - Gorton, Inv - Inverurie, Str - Stratford.
REPAIR CODES : C/H - Casual Heavy, **C/L** - Casual Light, **G** - General, **H** - Heavy, **H/I** - Heavy Intermediate, **L** - Light, **L/I** - Light Intermediate, **N/C** - Not classified.

E1555 ex-works in March 11th 1948 shows the painting style employed for the class by Stratford after nationalisation . The use of the letter prefix was brief, and was discontinued in that month. Photograph Rail Archive Stephenson.

A Stratford engine from 1920 until 1939, 8553 waits to ring off shed prior to working a down express from Liverpool Street. After the outbreak of war and the creation of a strong military presence in Essex, 8553 spent long periods at Colchester. Working to London and across country with troop trains to Peterborough and March. Relegated by the influx of B1 4-6-0s after the war, 8553 was sent to the Great Northern, working from Grantham between 1946 and 1957, returning to its native heath in the latter year to work its last year and a half from Cambridge.

1561 pilots B1 1271 at Shenfield in June 1948. After the war the LNER was restored to the tenders with yellow painted Gill Sans. Note the left hand toolbox has been removed. Photograph H.C.Casserley.

61557 on the Cambridge - Colchester line at Bartlow in June 1953. The engine is in unlined black with the BR emblem. Photograph L.R.Peters.

8500 with the black tar livery applied during the last war with N E only on the tender. Photographed at Keith circa 1944.

SHEDS:
Stratford.
Southend 17/5/30.
Stratford 9/8/30.
Southend 6/9/30.
Stratford 20/9/30.
Colchester 20/10/45.
Stratford 29/12/45.
Colchester 7/12/46.
Stratford 28/12/46.
Cambridge 10/2/57.

RENUMBERED:
1546 11/9/46.
61546 26/3/49.

CONDEMNED:
11/5/59.

8547

Beardmore 141.

To traffic 10/1920.

REPAIRS:
Str. 12/9/23-1/1/24.**G.** *Superior tube cleaner.*
Str. 2/5-14/8/25.**G.**
Str. 3/3-2/7/27.**G.** *Vac.brake added. Tube cleaner off.*
Str. 29/12/28-22/3/29.**G.** *Coal guard on tender.*
Str. 26/1-3/4/30.**G.**
Str. 23/3-30/5/31.**G.**
Str. 20/10-17/12/32.**G.**
Str. 3/5-29/6/34.**G.**
Str. 17/11/35-16/1/36.**G.**
Str. 21/5-8/7/37.**G.** *Reb to part 3.*
Str. 24/12/38-9/3/39.**G.**
Str. 28/7-4/10/40.**G.** *Footsteps alt.for ambulance trains.*
Str. 14/5-10/6/42.**L/I.**
Str. 7/6-25/9/43.**G.**
Str. 29/1-15/2/44.**N/C.**
Str. 27/3-7/4/44.**L.**
Str. 28/2-21/4/45.**G.**
Str. 6/2-27/3/47.**G.**
Str. 6-14/9/48.**N/C.**
Str. 12/6-23/7/49.**G.**
Str. 6/5-29/6/51.**G.**
Str. 21-29/8/51.**C/L.**
Str. 28/6-11/9/54.**G.**
Str. 17/12/56-2/2/57.**G.**
Str. 8/10/58.*Not repaired.*

BOILERS:
1547.
1525 (ex1536) 1/1/24.
1550 (ex1550) 14/8/25.
3846 (new) 22/3/29.
3822 (ex8552) 17/12/32.
3823 (ex8555) 29/6/34.
3827 (ex8560) 16/1/36.
4147 (new) 8/7/37.
4113 (ex8554) 9/3/39.
4126 (ex8523) 4/10/40.
4159 (ex8545) 25/9/43.
4106 (ex7470) 21/4/45.
4123 (ex1553) 27/3/47.
4154 (ex1540) 23/7/49.
27924 (ex1554) 29/6/51.
27952 (ex1549) 2/2/57.

SHEDS:
Stratford.
Norwich 12/9/24.
Stratford 13/10/24.
Colchester 20/10/45.
Stratford 29/12/45.
South Lynn 21/12/48.
Norwich 19/9/54.

RENUMBERED:
1547 10/9/46.
61547 11/9/48.

CONDEMNED:
13/10/58.

8548

Beardmore 143.

To traffic 4/1921.

REPAIRS:
Str. 17/5/21.**G.**
Str. 20/3-27/6/24.**G.**
Str. 11/25.**G.**
Str. 7/27.**G.** *Vac.brake.*
Str. 3/29.**G.** *Coal guard.*
Str. 25/4-19/6/30.**G.**
Str. 10/31.**G.** *ACFI on.*
Str. 5/33.**G.** *Tab.exch.*
Inv. 21/3/35.**H.**
Inv. 15/5/36.**H.**
Inv. 31/10/36.**G.**
Inv. 16/4/38.**H.**
Inv. 22/4/39.**H.**
Inv. 19/4/41.**G.**
Inv. 12/6/43.**G.**
Inv. 1/6/44.**L.**
Inv. 21/10/44.**L.**
Inv. 10/2-10/3/45.**H.**
Inv. 25/8-8/9/45.**L.**
Inv. 26/1-16/2/46.**G.**
Inv. 8-13/7/46.**N/C.**

BOILERS:
1548.
1544 (ex1569) 11/25.
3825 (new) 7/27.
1548 (ex8529) 3/29.
3859 (new) 19/6/30.
3833 (ex8522) 5/33.
Renumbered C1819 21/3/35.
3849 (exStr & 8512) 31/10/36.
3821 (ex8500) 19/4/41.
3841 (ex8508) 12/6/43.
3826 (ex8532) 16/2/46.

SHEDS:
Stratford.
Southend 26/7/30.
Stratford 8/9/30.
Kittybrewster 9/6/33.

RENUMBERED:
1548 31/3/46.

CONDEMNED:
28/12/46.

Instead of the letter prefix, the figure 6 was substituted, as shown by 61580, which was ex-works on May 8th 1948. Due to the wrong advice from Doncaster, figures 6 and 9 had curled tail, so were not true Gill Sans design, and it took some time for the corrections to take place.

Despite the LNER's declared intention to restore green livery it was slow in appearing from Stratford, but that works did exhaust its stocks of shaded transfers for figures and letters. Thompson decided they were too expensive to replenish, so they were replaced by yellow painted and unshaded Gill Sans type, 1542 acquiring them when ex-works in October 1947.

After nationalisation, Inverurie put another fourteen engines into LNER green together with the customary black and white lining. All had 10in. BRITISH RAILWAYS on tender, but still showing its individuality, Inverurie used only 8.5in. unshaded yellow painted figures for the cab numbering, although 61536 shows they were led adrift by Doncaster into using incorrect Gill Sans 6, 9. Photograph John Robertson.

The final BR (steam) crest was first applied to a B12 in April 1957 although only eight of the class were thus treated.

Once again, Stratford had some tidying up to do on liveries, but 61556 ex-works on December 1st 1948, showed that it could be done. Black with red, cream, and grey lining had been adopted as standard for this class, with the same size (10in.) figures and letters, painted at the same level. Note that the figure 6 now conforms to true Gill Sans. Front end number was also changed from painted display on the buffer beam to a cast iron plate mounted on the smokebox door. 61556 is at Colchester on April 16th 1949 with a stopping passenger train.

8549

Beardmore 144.

To traffic 6/1921.

REPAIRS:
Str. 30/1-17/3/23.**G.**
Str. 3/5-20/7/24.**G.**
Str. 5/3-3/9/26.**G.**
Str. 4/11/27-22/2/28.**G.** *Coal guard on tender.*
Str. 23/2-8/6/29.**G.**
Str. 1/11/30-4/2/31.**G.**
Str. 30/4-27/7/32.**G.** *ACFI fitted.*
Str. 27/12/33-22/2/34.**G.**
Str. 12/10-12/12/35.**G.**
Str. 10/2-1/4/37.**G.**
Str. 28/11/38-8/3/39.**G.**
Str. 4/10-1/11/40.**L.**
Str. 27/3-4/7/41.**G.** *ACFI removed.*
Str. 7/11/43-15/1/44.**G.** *Reb to pt 3.*
Str. 2-4/3/44.**N/C.**
Str. 21-22/4/44.**N/C.** *Ambulance valve.*
Str. 30/9-3/11/45.**G.** *Blow.down fitted.*
Str. 9/5-3/7/47.**G.**
Str. 14/11-26/12/48.**G.**
Str. 2-16/6/50.**C/L.**
Str. 31/12/50-17/2/51.**G.**
Str. 4/9-10/10/52.**G.**

Str. 16-28/7/53.**C/L.**
Str. 18/3-15/4/54.**C/L.**
Str. 8/11-11/12/54.**G.**
Str. 11/7-18/8/55.**C/L.**
Str. 9/2-11/4/56.**C/L.**
Str. 4/12/56-19/1/57.**G.**

BOILERS:
1549.
3809 *(ex8500)* 3/9/26.
3823 *(ex8562)* 22/2/28.
3809 *(ex8522)* 4/2/31.
1542 *(ex8540)* 27/7/32.
1574 *(ex8526)* 22/2/34.
1560 *(ex8272)* 12/12/35.
1576 *(ex8507)* 1/4/37.
1573 *(ex8563)* 8/3/39.
4161 (ex8530) 15/1/44.
4111 (ex8564) 3/11/45.
4100 (ex1517) 3/7/47.
4148 (ex1571) 26/12/48.
27911 (ex1569) 17/2/51.
27906 (ex1558) 10/10/52.
27952 *(new)* 11/12/54.
27902 (ex1514) 19/1/57.

SHEDS:
Stratford.
Southend 8/2/30.
Stratford 22/2/30.
Southend 23/8/30.
Stratford 6/9/30.

Parkeston 3/12/39.
Stratford 17/3/40.
Colchester 29/12/45.
Stratford 25/1/47.
Cambridge 10/2/57.

RENUMBERED:
1549 19/5/46.
61549 24/12/48.

CONDEMNED:
1/1/59.

8550

Beardmore 142.

To traffic 10/1920.

REPAIRS:
Str. 9/4-30/6/23.**G.**
Str. 20/10/24-3/4/25.**G.**
Str. 8/10/26-18/2/27.**G.** *Coal guard on tender.*
Str. 2/3-21/5/28.**G.** *Ashcroft cut-off control.*
Str. 28/12/28-8/1/29.**N/C.** *Flaman rec.fitted.*
Str. 12/10-19/12/29.**G.**
Str. 31/1-14/4/31.**G.** *Flaman rec.removed.*

Str. 25/6/31.**N/C.** *Flaman on.*
Str. 12/31. *Flaman off and put on B17 2800.*
Str. 28/1-7/4/33.**G.**
Str. 24/9/34-14/3/35.**G.**
Str. 12/3-15/5/36.**G.** *Reb to part 3.*
Str. 1/6-23/7/37.**G.**
Str. 17-23/9/38.**L.**
Str. 30/1-31/3/39.**G.**
Str. 29/12/39-18/1/40.**L.**
Str. 13/9/40-29/1/41.**G.**
Str. 14/11/42-30/1/43.**G.**
Str. 10/12/44-13/1/45.**G.**
Str. 22/10-17/11/45.**L.**
Str. 29/1-28/2/46.**L.**
Str. 9/1-10/3/47.**G.**
Str. 23/5-24/6/48.**L.**
Str. 5/12/48-14/1/49.**G.**
Str. 14/3-21/4/50.**C/H.**
Str. 30/6-1/8/50.**C/L.**
Str. 11/1-17/2/51.**H/I.**
Str. 2/7-2/8/52.**C/L.**
Str. 4/3-25/4/53.**G.**
Str. 14/3-4/6/55.**G.**
Str. 13-20/9/56.**N/C.**

BOILERS:
1550.
1502 *(ex1521)* 3/4/25.
1554 *(ex8554)* 18/2/27.
1540 *(ex8523)* 19/12/29.
3840 *(ex8285)* 7/4/33.

WORKS CODES : Cow - Cowlairs, Dar - Darlington, Don - Doncaster, Ghd - Gateshead, Gor - Gorton, Inv - Inverurie, Str - Stratford.
REPAIR CODES : **C/H** - Casual Heavy, **C/L** - Casual Light, **G** - General, **H** - Heavy, **H/I** - Heavy Intermediate, **L** - Light, **L/I** - Light Intermediate, **N/C** - Not classified.

3855 *(ex8518)* 14/3/35.
4118 *(ex8509)* 15/5/36.
4123 *(ex8574)* 23/7/37.
4130 *(ex8518)* 31/3/39.
4127 *(ex8554)* 29/1/41.
4136 *(ex spare & 8565)* 30/1/43.
4157 *(ex8571)* 13/1/45.
4104 *(ex1580)* 10/3/47.
4156 *(ex1514)* 14/1/49.
4163 *(ex1555)* 21/4/50.
Renumbered 27914 17/2/51.
27920 *(ex1577)* 25/4/53.
27911 *(ex1546)* 4/6/55.

SHEDS:
Stratford.
Ipswich 9/1/29.
Stratford 4/2/29.
Ipswich 13/4/29.
Stratford 18/4/29.
Southend 11/10/30.
Stratford 25/10/30.
Ipswich 19/7/35.
Stratford 31/10/35.
Colchester 20/7/41.
Stratford 10/8/41.

RENUMBERED:
1550 5/10/46.
61550 24/6/48.

CONDEMNED:
1/1/57.

8551

Beardmore 145.

To traffic 11/1920.

REPAIRS:
Str. 19/7-2/8/22.**L.**

Str. 5-7/24.**G.** *Vac.brake.*
Str. 10/26.**G.**
Str. 28/3-9/6/28.**G.** *Coal guard.*
Str. 6/29.**G.**
Str. 3/10-11/11/32.**G.**
Str. 3/34.**G.** *ACFI on.*
Str. 2/36.**G.**
Str. 6/37.**G.**
Str. 11/1/39.**G.**
Inv. 15/7/39.**H.** *Tab.exch.*
Inv. 15/6/40.**H.**
Inv. 14/9/40.**L.**
Inv. 2/8/41.**L.**
Inv. 13/12/41.**L.**
Inv. 31/1/42.**L.**
Inv. 22/8-12/9/42.**G.**
Inv. 13/1/43.**L.**
Inv. 13/8/43.**L.**
Inv. 18/11/43.**L.**
Inv. 22/4/44.**G.**
Inv. 24/2-3/3/45.**L.**
Inv. 23/6-2/8/45.**H.**
Inv. 14-17/11/45.**L.**

BOILERS:
1551.
1560 *(ex8560)* 10/26.
1543 *(ex8501)* 9/6/28.
1564 *(ex8542)* 6/29.
3800 *(ex8544)* 11/11/32.
3804 *(ex8544)* 3/34.
1572 *(ex8554)* 2/36.
3858 *(ex8534)* 6/37.
3842 *(ex8562)* 11/1/39.
3848 *(ex8503)* 12/9/42.
1288 *(ex8504)* 22/4/44.

SHEDS:
Stratford.
Southend 22/3/30.
Stratford 28/6/30.
Southend 18/10/30.
Stratford 25/10/30.

Parkeston 19/7/35.
Stratford 31/10/35.
Kittybrewster 31/5/39.
Eastfield 19/3/45.
Kittybrewster 31/7/45.

RENUMBERED:
1551 1/9/46.

CONDEMNED:
17/1/47.

8552

Beardmore 146.

To traffic 12/1920.

REPAIRS:
Str. 16/10/23-26/1/24.**G.**
Vac.brake.
Str. 3/26.**G.**
Str. 1-3/28.**G.** *Coal guard.*
Str. 24/10-11/12/29.**G.**
Str. 10/32.**G.**
Str. 4/34.**G.** *ACFI on.*
Str. 11/35.**G.**
Str. 3/37.**G.**
Str. 19/1/39.**G.**
Inv. 16/9/39.**N/C.** *Tab.exch.*
Inv. 12/10/40.**H.**
Inv. 30/5/42.**H.**
Inv. 6/2/43.**G.**
Inv. 25/2/43.**L.**
Inv. 27/4/43.**L.**
Inv. 22/6/43.**L.**
Inv. 3/7/43.**L.**
Inv. 20/8/43.**L.**
Inv. 15/4/44.**G.**
Inv. 19-20/10/44.**N/C.**
Inv. 7/12/44.**L.**
Inv. 3/11-8/12/45.**H.**

Inv. 6-13/7/46.**L.**
Inv. 23/11-14/12/46.**G.**
Inv. 2/9-16/10/48.**G.**
Inv. 15/3/50.**L.**
Inv. 16/6/51.**G.**

BOILERS:
1552.
3803 *(ex1570)* 26/1/24.
1515 *(ex8563)* 3/26.
1532 *(ex8539)* 3/28.
3822 *(ex8537)* 11/12/29.
1565 *(ex8560)* 10/32.
1578 *(ex8577)* 4/34.
1274 *(ex8505)* 11/35.
1579 *(ex8522)* 3/37.
1571 *(ex8521)* 19/1/39.
C1777 *(ex8536)* 30/5/42.
3840 *(ex8507)* 15/4/44.
3829 *(ex8560)* 14/12/46.
3841 *(ex1501)* 16/10/48.
23111 *(ex61502)* 16/6/51.

SHEDS:
Ipswich.
Copley Hill 4/24.
Ipswich 7/24.
Stratford 27/3/26.
Kittybrewster 16/7/39.
Eastfield 26/3/45.
Kittybrewster 31/7/45.

RENUMBERED:
1552 20/10/46.
61552 16/10/48.

CONDEMNED:
17/7/52.

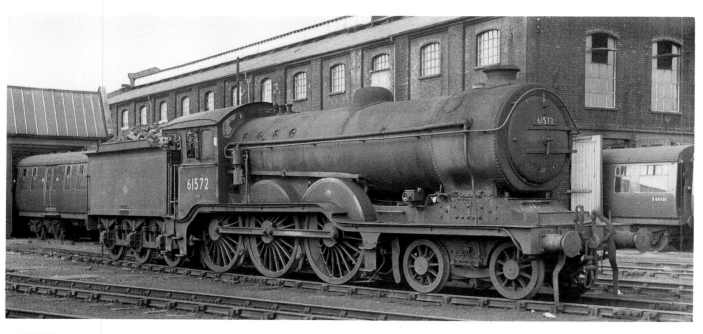

In 1956 B.R. were awarded a grant of arms, and from it, decided to use the crest instead of the emblem. Mistakenly, handed transfers were ordered for it, so that the lion could still face forward on both sides, thus incurring the Heralds' displeasure, and consequent correction. From August 31st 1957 to March 22nd 1958, eight B12/3s had crests put on, all of them with the lion facing the wrong way on the right hand side. By late 1958, correction was being made on other classes, but no B12/3 received further repair, and all were withdrawn whilst still in disgrace with the College of Heralds. 61572 had the crests from February 14th 1958 to its September 1961 demise.

8532 ex-works on January 19th 1946 showed L N E R restored, and when the number was changed to 1532 on August 11th 1946, the works were still able to find shaded transfers.

Inverurie continued applying black paint during the war but ceased to put any lining on it, and from 1942 only put N E on the tender. These two initials continued until well into 1946, and after renumbering 1502 still had them, although ex-works and duly renumbered on August 30th 1947, as here at Kittybrewster on October 16th 1947. Photograph H.C.Casserley.

Changing of tenders could lead to some unlikely combinations. Engine 61552 ex-works in June 1951 had been duly painted in BR lined black, and with correct Gill Sans 6, but from April 1952 it had been paired with a green painted B17 tender No.2803, which Darlington had sent . They remained coupled until 61552's withdrawal on July 17th 1952.

8553

Beardmore 147.

To traffic 12/1920.

REPAIRS:
Str. 9/1-16/6/23.**G**.
Str. 18/9/24-25/2/25.**G**.
Str. 22/10/26-19/2/27.**G**. *Coal guard on tender.*
Str. 8/27.**N/C**. *Vac.brake.*
Str. 3/2-20/4/28.**G**.
Str. 6/4-15/7/29.**G**.
Str. 4/10-22/12/30.**G**.
Str. 26/3-10/6/32.**G**. *ACFI fitted.*
Str. 15-19/8/32.**L**.
Str. 11/1-9/3/34.**G**.
Str. 25/9-15/11/35.**G**.
Str. 28/11-20/12/35.**L**.
Str. 13/12/36-6/1/37.**L**.
Str. 20/3-21/5/37.**G**. *Reb to part 3.*
Str. 26/2-4/3/38.**L**.
Str. 21-29/4/38.**L**.
Str. 28/8-24/10/38.**G**.
Str. 26/7-8/8/39.**L**.
Str. 7/3-3/5/40.**G**.
Str. 7/11-6/12/40.**L**.
Str. 18/10-23/11/42.**G**.
Str. 5-10/12/42.**L**.
Str. 10-14/3/44.**N/C**. *Ambulance valve.*
Str. 10/9-14/10/44.**G**.

Str. 10/11-28/12/46.**G**.
Str. 13/1-2/3/48.**L**.
Str. 2/1-16/2/49.**G**.
Str. 23/8-24/9/49.**C/L**.
Str. 22/10-5/11/49.**C/L**.
Str. 24/5-23/6/50.**C/L**.
Str. 22/4-13/6/51.**G**.
Str. 5/3-11/4/53.**G**.
Str. 10/6-18/8/56.**G**.
Str. 24/8-1/9/56.**N/C**.

BOILERS:
1553.
1530 *(ex1502)* 16/6/23.
1517 *(ex1510)* 25/2/25.
1552 *(ex8561)* 19/2/27.
1565 *(ex8560)* 20/4/28.
1539 *(ex8525)* 22/12/30.
3847 *(ex8569)* 10/6/32.
1285 *(ex8543)* 9/3/34.
1542 *(ex8523)* 15/11/35.
4144 *(new)* 21/5/37.
4104 *(ex8572)* 24/10/38.
4139 *(ex8555)* 3/5/40.
4147 *(ex8525)* 23/11/42.
4123 *(ex8510)* 14/10/44.
4102 *(ex7479)* 28/12/46.
4100 *(ex1549)* 16/2/49.
27923 *(ex1578)* 13/6/51.
27936 *(ex1523)* 11/4/53.
27908 *(ex1566)* 18/8/56.

SHEDS:

Stratford.
Colchester 25/9/39.
Stratford 3/12/39.
Colchester 16/10/43.
Stratford 8/1/44.
Colchester 11/11/44.
Stratford 7/12/46.
Colchester 28/12/46.
Stratford 10/4/49.
Grantham 11/12/49.
Cambridge 24/3/57.

RENUMBERED:
7467 28/11/42.
1553 22/9/46.
61553 5/11/49.

CONDEMNED:
25/8/58.

8554

Beardmore 148.

To traffic 1/1921.

REPAIRS:
Str. 7/11/22-3/3/23.**G**.
Str. 19/2-3/6/24.**G**.
Str. 5/3-3/9/26.**G**.
Str. 13/8-7/12/28.**G**. *Coal guard on tender.*

Str. 7/2-7/4/30.**G**.
Str. Stood 2/1-3/5/32.*
Str. 3/5-18/8/32.**G**. *ACFI fitted.*
Str. 28/12/33-23/2/34.**G**.
Str. 24/9-8/11/35.**G**. *Reb to part 3.*
Str. 7/1-26/2/37.**G**.
Str. 1-12/8/37.**L**.
Str. 31/8-6/9/37.**L**.
Str. 9-19/8/38.**L**.
Str. 15/11/38-9/2/39.**G**.
Str. 26/7-19/10/40.**G**. *Footsteps alt.for ambulance trains.*
Str. 2-14/11/41.**L**.
Str. 18/7-22/8/42.**G**.
Str. 2-8/10/42.**L**.
Str. 3/1-26/2/44.**G**.
Str. 4-7/4/44.**N/C**. *Ambulance valve.*
Str. 12-30/6/45.**G**.
Str. 2/3-1/5/47.**G**.
Str. 14-15/10/48.**N/C**.
Str. 28/11/48-11/1/49.**G**.
Str. 9-17/3/49.**C/L**.
Str. 24/1-3/5/50.**C/L**.
Str. 17/12/50-10/2/51.**G**.
Str. 4/12/52-6/2/53.**G**.
Str. 24/1-10/3/55.**G**.
Str. 4/8-10/9/55.**C/L**. *After collision.*

BOILERS:
1554.
1520 *(ex1537)* 3/9/26.

WORKS CODES : Cow - Cowlairs, Dar - Darlington, Don - Doncaster, Ghd - Gateshead, Gor - Gorton, Inv - Inverurie, Str - Stratford.
REPAIR CODES : **C/H** - Casual Heavy, **C/L** - Casual Light, **G** - General, **H** - Heavy, **H/I** - Heavy Intermediate, **L** - Light, **L/I** - Light Intermediate, **N/C** - Not classified.

65

3842 *(new)* 7/12/28.
1273 *(ex8505)* 18/8/32.
1572 *(ex8520)* 23/2/34.
4128 *(new)* 8/11/35.
4113 *(ex8569)* 26/2/37.
4127 *(ex8544)* 9/2/39.
4119 *(ex8578)* 19/10/40.
4114 *(ex spare & 8535)* 22/8/42.
4121 *(ex8579)* 26/2/44.
4109 *(ex8575)* 30/6/45.
4106 *(ex1547)* 1/5/47.
4161 *(ex1530)* 11/1/49.
27912 *(ex1556)* 10/2/51.
27910 *(ex1578)* 6/2/53.
27941 *(ex1555)* 10/3/55.

SHEDS:
Stratford.
Southend 26/4/30.
Stratford 26/7/30.
Southend 15/11/30.
Stratford 2/1/32.
Grantham 18/12/49.
Peterborough 4/3/56.
Cambridge 24/3/57.

RENUMBERED:
1554 31/10/46.
61554 8/1/49.

CONDEMNED:
15/9/58.

*This engine was concerned in the fire at Littlebury in June 1931 and was standing at Stratford works awaiting examination by the plaintiffs.

8555

Beardmore 149.

To traffic 12/1920.

REPAIRS:
Str. 17/10/22-30/6/23.**G.**
Str. 15/10/24-10/2/25.**G.**
Str. 9/12/26-4/3/27.**G.** *Vac.brake added.*

Str. 6/5-13/7/28.**G.** *Coal guard on tender.*
Str. 14/10/29-2/1/30.**G.**
Str. 21/2-30/4/31.**G.**
Str. 11/10-12/12/32.**G.**
Str. 8/4-11/6/34.**G.**
Str. 20-28/6/35.**L.**
Str. 3/9-24/10/35.**G.** *Reb to part 3.*
Str. 3/1-12/2/37.**G.**
Str. 28/5-7/7/38.**G.**
Str. 7-17/6/39.**L.**
Str. 16/10-22/12/39.**G.**
Str. 20/9-31/10/41.**G.**
Str. 12/2-17/3/44.**G.**
Str. 5/4-44.**N/C.** *Ambulance valve.*
Str. 2/12/45-12/1/46.**G.**
Str. 31/12/46-1/2/47.**L.**
Str. 12/1-11/3/48.**G.**
Str. 10-26/8/49.**C/L.**
Str. 4-21/9/49.**C/L.**
Str. 8/12/49-28/1/50.**G.**
Str. 2/6-11/8/50.**C/L.**
Str. 31/3-16/5/52.**G.**
Str. 22/1-21/2/53.**N/C.**
Str. 22/11/54-8/1/55.**G.**
Str. 19/9/57.*Not repaired.*

BOILERS:
1555.
1558 *(ex8558)* 4/3/27.
3823 *(ex8549)* 30/4/31.
1579 *(ex8505)* 11/6/34.
4127 *(new)* 24/10/35.
4109 *(ex8576)* 12/2/37.
4139 *(ex8569)* 7/7/38.
4152 *(ex8562)* 22/12/39.
4154 *(ex8540)* 31/10/41.
4114 *(ex8554)* 17/3/44.
4127 *(ex8515)* 12/1/46.
4163 *(ex1538)* 11/3/48.
4150 *(ex1515)* 28/1/50.
27941 *(ex1567)* 16/5/52.
27947 *(ex1545)* 8/1/55.

SHEDS:
Stratford.
Parkeston 4/3/27.
Ipswich 13/1/28.
Colchester 18/7/28.
Stratford 21/5/29.
Southend 1/2/30.

Stratford 16/7/30.
Southend 2/8/30.
Stratford 13/9/30.
Colchester 1/2/48.
Stratford 13/12/53.
Colchester 28/10/56.
Grantham 6/1/57.
Cambridge 24/3/57.

RENUMBERED:
1555 13/9/46.
E1555 11/3/48.
61555 10/9/49.

CONDEMNED:
7/10/57.

8556

Beardmore 150.

To traffic 2/1921.

REPAIRS:
Str. 17/3-9/6/23.**G.**
Str. 3/5-19/7/24.**G.**
Str. 13/11/25-15/4/26.**G.**
Str. 1/4-16/7/27.**G.**
Str. 2/11/28-15/3/29.**G.** *Vac.brake & coal guard on tender.*
Str. 7/3-12/5/30.**G.**
Str. 17/10/31-1/1/32.**G.** *ACFI fitted.*
Str. 2/10-1/12/33.**G.**
Str. 16/5-6/6/34.**H.**
Str. 11/3-24/5/35.**G.** *Reb to part 3.*
Str. 28/9-5/11/36.**G.**
Str. 24/8-3/9/37.**L.**
Str. 9/11-22/12/37.**G.**
Str. 26/3-1/6/39.**G.**
Str. 9/11/40-9/1/41.**G.**
Str. 11/2-24/3/41.**L.**
Str. 5-18/11/42.**G.**
Str. 21/2-8/5/43.**G.**
Str. 13-25/9/43.**L.**
Str. 7/1-4/3/44.**G.**
Str. 18/2-24/3/45.**G.**
Str. 22/5-1/8/46.**G.**
Str. 17/8-22/9/47.**L.**
Str. 25/10-1/12/48.**G.**

Str. 17/1-23/2/49.**L.**
Str. 12-21/5/49.**C/L.**
Str. 5-19/8/49.**C/L.**
Str. 11/10-11/11/50.**G.**
Str. 13/10-6/12/52.**G.**
Str. 6/6-12/8/55.**G.**
Str. 7-29/6/56.**C/L.**
Str. 20/11/56-19/1/57.**C/L.**

BOILERS:
1556.
1535 *(ex8535)* 15/4/26.
3803 *(ex8568)* 12/5/30.
1549 *(ex8562)* 1/1/32.
1541 *(ex8511)* 1/12/33.
4100 *(ex8579)* 24/5/35.
4102 *(ex8540)* 5/11/36.
4135 *(ex8519)* 22/12/37.
4131 *(ex8533)* 1/6/39.
4113 *(ex8547)* 9/1/41.
4106 *(ex8516)* 8/5/43.
4146 *(ex7482)* 24/3/45.
4108 *(ex7472)* 1/8/46.
4149 *(ex1558)* 1/12/48.
27905 *(ex1535)* 11/11/50.
27926 *(ex1512)* 6/12/52.
27920 *(ex1550)* 12/8/55.

SHEDS:
Stratford.
Ipswich 15/12/27.
Colchester 14/1/28.
Norwich 13/3/29.
Stratford 23/5/29.
Colchester 16/10/43.
Stratford 8/1/44.
Colchester 11/11/44.
Stratford 8/2/47.
Colchester 1/2/48.
Stratford 13/12/53.
Colchester 28/10/56.
Norwich 6/1/57.

RENUMBERED:
7470 21/11/42.
1556 17/11/46.
61556 27/11/48.

CONDEMNED:
23/12/57.

Although a terrible photograph, the instances of B12s being piloted by a Great Western locomotive were rare to say the least. In this view 8525 has a Hall 4-6-0 as an assistant whilst working a wartime ambulance train.

61514 runs into Wisbech with a Kings Lynn - March service in June 1959.

1577 (formerly 8577) waiting to leave Liverpool Street with a down express. The ten built in 1928 did not have the traversing provision for the rear coupled axle, yet 1577 has acquired coupling rods with hinge and square-ended bush which that feature needed. This appeared whilst in works waiting to be fitted with new cylinders and represented something of an oddity in detail. Photograph Rail Archive Stephenson.

8502 has acquired fully lined green livery in this 1929 view at Beccles, where it is to work a slow passenger train to Cromer.

8557

Beardmore 151.

To traffic 3/1921.

REPAIRS:
Str. 24/4-2/8/23.**G.**
Str. 24/10/24-16/4/25.**G.**
Str. 4/11/26-2/4/27.**G.** *Vac.brake.*
Coal guard on tender.
Str. 15/9-11/12/28.**G.**
Str. 13/9-5/11/29.**L.**
Str. 21/2-2/5/30.**G.**
Str. 27/3-27/6/31.**G.**
Str. 3/11-30/12/32.**G.**
Str. 4-15/9/33.**L.**
Str. 22/10-20/12/34.**G.** *Reb to pt 3.*
Str. 27/1-12/3/36.**G.**
Str. 12/4-18/6/37.**G.**
Str. 12/9-28/10/38.**G.**
Str. 6/2-12/4/40.**G.**
Str. 5-12/10/40.**L.**
Str. 9/1-21/2/42.**G.**
Str. 11/2-18/3/44.**G.**
Str. 21-22/4/44.**N/C.** *Ambulance*
valve.
Str. 19/5-3/6/44.**L.**

Str. 7/9-27/10/45.**G.** *Blow down*
fitted.
Str. 6/5-29/6/47.**G.** *Blow down*
removed.
Str. 18/11/49-7/1/50.**G.**
Str. 23/9-26/10/51.**G.**
Str. 10/3-4/9/53.**C/L.**
Str. 1/7-18/9/54.**G.**

BOILERS:
1557.
1546 *(ex1546)* 16/4/25.
1557 *(ex8521)* 11/12/28.
1534 *(ex8510)* 2/5/30.
1559 *(ex8558)* 27/6/31.
3861 *(ex8517)* 30/12/32.
4120 *(new)* 20/12/34.
4131 *(new)* 12/3/36.
4110 *(ex8540)* 18/6/37.
4100 *(ex8535)* 28/10/38.
4150 *(ex8530)* 12/4/40.
4108 *(ex8572)* 21/2/42.
4142 *(ex7479)* 18/3/44.
4133 *(ex8533)* 27/10/45.
4119 *(ex1578)* 29/6/47.
4132 *(ex1579)* 7/1/50.
27931 *(ex1533)* 26/10/51.
27950 *(new)* 18/9/54.

SHEDS:
Stratford.
Ardsley 4/24.
Stratford 8/24.
Gorton 18/4/27.
Parkeston 20/4/28.
Stratford 14/12/28.
Colchester 22/2/41.
Stratford 13/4/41.
Colchester 29/12/45.
Stratford 25/1/47.
Colchester 1/2/48.
Stratford 13/12/53.
Colchester 28/10/56.

RENUMBERED:
1557 6/10/46.
61557 7/1/50.

CONDEMNED:
1/1/57.

8558

Beardmore 152.

To traffic 3/1921.

REPAIRS:
Str. 2/10/22-6/1/23.**G.** *West.3 stage*
brake pump put on.
Str. 15/1-13/6/24.**G.** *West.3 stage*
compressor replaced by vac.brake.
Str. 15/4-15/10/26.**G.**
Str. 27/3-20/6/28.**G.** *Coal guard on*
tender.
Str. 2/11/29-17/1/30.**G.**
Str. 14/2-10/4/31.**G.**
Str. 19/9-8/11/32.**G.**
Str. 8/3-3/5/34.**G.**
Str. 20/9-15/11/35.**G.** *Reb to pt 3.*
Str. 26/1-6/3/36.**H.**
Str. 21/2-15/4/37.**G.**
Str. 21-31/5/37.**L.**
Str. 22/10-30/12/38.**G.**
Str. 7/4-24/5/40.**G.**
Str. 26/7-10/10/40.**L.** *Footsteps*
alt.for ambulance trains.
Str. 4/3-27/4/42.**G.**
Str. 22-31/7/42.**L.**
Str. 15/12/42-5/1/43.**L.**
Str. 15/4-13/5/44.**L.**
Str. 14-28/7/45.**L.**
Str. 3/3-16/4/46.**G.**
Str. 2/5-16/6/48.**G.**
Str. 9/2-8/4/50.**G.**
Str. 27/10-4/11/50.**C/L.**

WORKS CODES : Cow - Cowlairs, Dar - Darlington, Don - Doncaster, Ghd - Gateshead, Gor - Gorton, Inv - Inverurie, Str - Stratford.
REPAIR CODES : **C/H** - Casual Heavy, **C/L** - Casual Light, **G** - General, **H** - Heavy, **H/I** - Heavy Intermediate, **L** - Light, **L/I** - Light Intermediate, **N/C** - Not classified.

Str. 8/5-24/6/52.**G.**
Str. 30/4-7/5/53.**C/L.**
Str. 26/7-3/9/55.**G.**
Str. 16/8-13/9/56.**C/L.**
Str. 29/9-23/11/57.**G.**
Str. 24/3-30/5/58.**N/C.**

BOILERS:
1558.
1272 *(ex8532)* 15/10/26.
1559 *(ex8500)* 20/6/28.
1544 *(ex8517)* 10/4/31.
1576 *(ex8576)* 8/11/32.
1565 *(ex8552)* 3/5/34.
4129 *(new)* 15/11/35.
4128 *(ex8554)* 15/4/37.
4146 *(ex8523)* 30/12/38.
4144 *(ex8542)* 24/5/40.
4140 *(ex8515)* 27/4/42.
4108 *(ex8557)* 13/5/44.
4149 *(ex8530)* 16/4/46.
4127 *(ex1555)* 16/6/48.
4141 *(ex1564)* 8/4/50.
Renumbered 27906 4/11/50.
27944 *(ex1580)* 24/6/52.
27949 *(ex1516)* 3/9/55.
27911 *(ex1550)* 23/11/57.

SHEDS:
Stratford.
Ipswich 15/10/26.
Stratford 31/12/26.
Colchester 20/10/45.
Stratford 8/2/47.
Colchester 1/2/48.
Stratford 13/12/53.
Colchester 28/10/56.
Peterborough 6/1/57.
Cambridge 24/2/57.
Kings Lynn 7/4/57.
Cambridge 24/11/57.

RENUMBERED:
7472 5/1/43.
1558 6/10/46.
61558 12/6/48.

CONDEMNED:
13/4/59.

8559

Beardmore 153**.**

To traffic 3/1921.

REPAIRS:
Str. 11/12/22-29/3/23.**G.**
Str. 26/2-30/6/24.**G.**
Str. 13/1-1/5/26.**G.**
Str. 22/9/27-21/1/28.**G.** *Coal guard on tender.*
Str. 5-12/5/28.**N/C.** *Vac.brake fitted.*
Str. 16/3-5/6/29.**G.**
Str. 27/9-13/12/30.**G.** *Long travel valves fitted.*
Str. 10/2-21/3/31.**L.**
Str. 11-15/8/31.**L.**
Str. 21-24/3/32.**L.**
Str. 29/11/32-3/2/33.**G.**
Str. 28/4-9/5/33.**L.**
Str. 15/11/34-25/1/35.**G.**
Str. 8/3-1/5/36.**G.** *Rebuilt to part 3.*
Str. 26/5-1/7/37.**G.**
Str. 8-21/3/38.**L.**
Str. 23/9-20/10/38.**L.**
Str. 25/1-30/3/39.**G.**
Str. 3-19/4/40.**L.**
Str. 31/5-7/6/40.**L.**
Str. 15/7-3/8/40.**L.**
Str. 10/12/40-7/2/41.**G.**
Str. 6/12/42-25/1/43.**G.**
Str. 28/10-20/11/43.**L.**
Str. 29/2-3/3/44.**N/C.**
Str. 8/12/44-25/1/45.**G.**
Str. 17/2-16/3/46.**G.**
Str. 22/5-11/9/46.**L.**
Str. 3/1-20/2/48.**G.**
Str. 1-14/8/48.**L.**
Str. 31/3-21/5/49.**G.**

Str. 22/8-3/9/49.**C/L.**
Str. 2/3-20/4/50.**C/L.**
Str. 2/5-10/6/50.**C/L.**
Str. 23/8/51.*Not repaired.*

BOILERS:
1559.
1545 *(ex1545)* 1/5/26.
3848 *(new)* 5/6/29.
1564 *(ex8551)* 3/2/33.
3861 *(ex8557)* 25/1/35.
4105 *(ex8523)* 1/5/36.
4125 *(ex8523)* 1/7/37.
4148 *(ex8580)* 30/3/39.
4158 *(new)* 7/2/41.
4132 *(ex8580)* 25/1/43.
4126 *(ex spare & 8547)* 25/1/45.
4138 *(ex8510)* 16/3/46.
4105 *(ex1516)* 20/2/48.
4128 *(ex1561)* 21/5/49.

SHEDS:
Stratford.
Colchester 20/5/51.

RENUMBERED:
1559 20/7/46.
E1559 20/2/48.
61559 14/8/48.

CONDEMNED:
3/9/51.

8560

Beardmore 154.

To traffic 4/1921.

REPAIRS:
Str. 4-6/24.**G.**
Str. 11/2-8/7/26.**G.**
Str. 2/28.**G.** *Coal guard.*
Str. 5/28.**N/C.** *Vac.brake.*
Str. 2/31.**G.**

Str. 9/11/32.**G.** *ACFI on.*
Str. 3/34.**G.**
Str. 12/35.**G.**
Str. 5/37.**G.**
Str. 23/12/38.**G.**
Inv. 29/4/39.**N/C.** *Tab.exch.*
Inv. 8/12/39.**L.**
Inv. 29/6/40.**L.**
Inv. 18/1-22/2/41.**H.** *ACFI off.*
Inv. 29/3/41.**L.**
Inv. 23/3/42.**L.**
Inv. 26/12/42-16/1/43.**G.**
Inv. 23/8/43.**L.**
Inv. 3/12/43.**L.**
Inv. 24/6/44.**H.**
Inv. 20/10/44.**L.**
Inv. 7-21/4/45.**L.**
Inv. 19/1-19/2/46.**G.**
Inv. 11/7/46.**L.**
Inv. 24-28/9/46.**L.**
Inv. 27-28/2/47.**N/C.**
Inv. 29/9-2/10/48.**L.**
Inv. 15/1-5/2/49.**G.**
Inv. 9-23/12/50.**G.**

BOILERS:
1560.
1565 *(ex8566)* 8/7/26.
3829 *(new)* 2/28.
1565 *(ex8553)* 2/31.
1580 *(ex8580)* 9/11/32.
3827 *(ex8534)* 3/34.
1293 *(ex8563)* 12/35.
3832 *(ex8505)* 5/37.
3824 *(ex8512)* 23/12/38.
3829 *(ex8528)* 16/1/43.
3848 *(ex8529)* 19/2/46.
1572 *(ex1531)* 5/2/49.
23108 *(ex spare & 1560)* 23/12/50.

SHEDS:
Stratford.
Southend 27/9/30.
Stratford 4/10/30.
Kittybrewster 21/3/39.

RENUMBERED:
1560 1/9/46.
61560 2/10/48.

CONDEMNED:
9/5/52.

When 61562 was withdrawn from stock in August 1955 it was deliberately de-railed at Stratford as part of a demonstration of re-railing equipment.

7437 was the number that 8523 took on November 14th 1942 in the aborted Thompson re-numbering. Here at Stratford shed in June 1946 it is within a month of entering the works for a general repair from which it emerged with the number 1523, its original when built in May 1914.

From August 1949 BRITISH RAILWAYS ceased to be applied and was supplanted by this emblem of a lion straddling a wheel, which was handed to face forward on both sides of the tender. 61557 was ex-works with emblem on January 7th 1950, at Liverpool Street station with discs indicating a Southend train. Photograph S.M.Watkins.

8561

Stratford.

To traffic 4/1920.

REPAIRS:
Str. 25/10/23-5/3/24.**G.** *Vac.brake.*
Str. 20/3-18/9/26.**G.**
Str. 19-26/10/26.**L.**
Str. 22/2-2/4/27.**G.**
Str. 9/5-26/7/28.**G.** *Coal guard on tender.*
Str. 12-20/9/28.**L.**
Str. 28/12/29-6/3/30.**G.**
Str. 30/5-4/6/30.**L.**
Str. 24/1-7/4/31.**G.**
Str. 10/11/32-13/1/33.**G.**
Str. 1/5-22/6/34.**G.**
Str. 30/12/35-17/2/36.**G.**
Str. 14/2-9/4/37.**G.** *Reb to part 3.*
Str. 21-28/7/37.**L.**
Str. 6/11/38-26/1/39.**G.**
Str. 15/6-7/8/40.**G.**
Str. 27/12/41-31/1/42.**L.**
Str. 26/7-11/9/42.**G.**
Str. 24/10-23/11/43.**L.**
Str. 30/4-3/6/44.**G.**
Str. 31/7-25/8/45.**L.**
Str. 14/10-10/11/45.**G.**
Str. 1-19/2/46.**L.**
Str. 26/2-8/4/46.**L.**
Str. 7/6-1/9/47.**G.**
Str. 12/12/48-22/1/49.**G.**
Str. 11/4-5/5/50.**G.**
Str. 9/3-26/4/52.**G.**
Str. 28/3-8/5/54.**G.**
Str. 30/10-10/12/55.**G.**
Str. 1/10/56-17/1/57.**C/L.**
Str. 10-19/12/57.**C/L.**

BOILERS:
1561.
1552 *(ex1552)* 5/3/24.
1523 *(ex8528)* 18/9/26.
3801 *(ex8543)* 26/7/28.
1272 *(ex8270)* 7/4/31.
3828 *(ex8516)* 13/1/33.
3808 *(ex8522)* 22/6/34.
1574 *(ex8549)* 17/2/36.
4143 *(new)* 9/4/37.
4128 *(ex8558)* 26/1/39.
4146 *(ex8558)* 7/8/40.
4153 *(ex8544)* 11/9/42.
4141 *(ex8515)* 3/6/44.
4137 *(ex7449)* 10/11/45.
4128 *(ex1567)* 1/9/47.
4129 *(ex1509)* 22/1/49.
4151 *(ex1580)* 5/5/50.
27940 *(ex1566)* 26/4/52.
27928 *(ex1533)* 8/5/54.
27901 *(ex1573)* 10/12/55.

SHEDS:
Ipswich.
Ardsley 4/24.
Doncaster 27/2/25.
Ipswich 15/10/25.
Parkeston 1/1/29.
Stratford 5/6/29.
Norwich 27/5/43.
Yarmouth 30/5/43.
Norwich 12/12/43.
Yarmouth 6/8/44.
Norwich 22/10/44.
Ipswich 14/1/45.
Yarmouth 28/9/45.
Ipswich 3/9/47.

RENUMBERED:
1561 24/10/46.
61561 22/1/49.

CONDEMNED:
30/9/58.

8562

Stratford.

To traffic 4/1920.

REPAIRS:
Str. 10-19/7/23.**G.**
Str. 2/5-30/7/24.**G.**
Str. 16/1-28/2/25.**L.**
Str. 15/1-20/5/26.**G.**
Str. 17/9/27-18/1/28.**G.** *Coal guard on tender.*
Str. 25/1-6/2/29.**N/C.** *Vac.brake added.*
Str. 5/10-17/12/29.**G.**
Str. 12/3-23/5/31.**G.**
Str. 14/10-22/12/32.**G.**
Str. 16/2-20/4/34.**G.**
Str. 22/5-11/7/35.**G.**
Str. 3/7-31/8/36.**G.**
Str. 23/2-14/4/38.**G.** *Reb to part 3.*
Str. 18/9-16/11/39.**G.**
Str. 20/10-29/11/41.**G.**
Str. 19-28/3/42.**L.**
Str. 5-12/12/42.**L.**
Str. 23/5-7/8/43.**G.**
Str. 19/3-24/4/44.**L.**
Str. 4-26/9/44.**L.**
Str. 12/3-2/6/45.**G.**
Str. 29/12/46-12/2/47.**G.**
Str. 29/5-20/6/47.**L.**
Str. 4/7-1/9/48.**G.**
Str. 30/12/49-4/2/50.**G.**
Str. 8/8-8/9/51.**G.**
Str. 4/8-26/9/53.**G.**
Str. 26/7/55.*Not repaired.*

BOILERS:
1562.
3823 *(new)* 19/7/23.
1562 *(ex8570)* 18/1/28.
1549 *(ex8525)* 17/12/29.
1555 *(ex8565)* 23/5/31.
1547 *(ex8517)* 20/4/34.
3826 *(ex8526)* 11/7/35.
3842 *(ex8546)* 31/8/36.
4152 *(new)* 14/4/38.
4107 *(ex8541)* 16/11/39.
4123 *(ex8514)* 29/11/41.
4105 *(ex8544)* 7/8/43.
4129 *(ex8570)* 2/6/45.
4130 *(ex1573)* 12/2/47.
4138 *(ex8559)* 1/9/48.
4130 *(ex1512)* 4/2/50.
27927 *(ex1553)* 8/9/51.
27932 *(ex1573)* 26/9/53.

SHEDS:
Ipswich.
Norwich 19/6/25.
Ipswich 18/1/28.
Colchester 23/1/28.
Stratford 3/6/29.
Parkeston 31/5/30.
Ipswich 28/5/31.
Stratford 13/7/35.
Ipswich 31/10/35.

RENUMBERED:
7476 12/12/42.
1562 21/7/46.
61562 28/8/48.

CONDEMNED:
8/8/55.

8505 was one of the trio upon which the A.C.F.I. heater was first tried, and here in 1928 the engine is coming out of Lowestoft with what is clearly a slow passenger train although , the combination of disc and lamp is that which normally indicated a Class A fish, meat, fruit, or cattle train.

61513 calls at Maud Junction with the 12.25 Aberdeen - Peterhead on 6 June 1950. The stock of the train was formed of Great North vehicles, 7133, 7836 and 7421. Photograph W.A.Camwell.

8563

Stratford.

To traffic 4/1920.

REPAIRS:
Str. 30/1-28/2/22.**L.**
Str. 2/11/22-2/3/23.**G.**
Str. 6/24.**G.** *Vac.brake.*
Str. 16/2/26.**G.**
Str. 3/28.**G.** *Coal guard.*
Str. 11/29-1/30.**G.**
Str. 9/32. **G.** *ACFI on.*
Str. 3/34.**G.**
Str. 11/35.**G.**
Str. 12/36.**G.**
Str. 3/2/39.**G.**
Str. 20/5/39.**L.**
Inv. 12/9/40.**L.** *ACFI off.*
Inv. 12/6/41.**L.**
Inv. 11/10/41.**G.**
Inv. 28/11/42.**H.**
Inv. 15/5/43.**G.**
Inv. 17/9/43.**L.**
Inv. 12/1/44.**L.**
Inv. 19/2/44.**L.**
Inv. 8/7-19/8/44.**G.**
Inv. 23/11/44.**L.**
Inv. 15/3/45.**L.**
Inv. 23/2-13/4/46.**G.**
Inv. 13/7/46.**L.**
Inv. 17-24/8/46.**L.**
Inv. 15/3-17/4/48.**H.**
Inv. 15/5/50.**L.**
Inv. 27/6-27/7/51.**G.**
Inv. 28-31/7/52.**N/C.**

Inv. 20-21/11/52.**N/C.**
Inv. 23/3/53.*Not repaired.*

BOILERS:
1563.
1515 *(ex1512)* 2/3/23.
1505 *(ex8507)* 16/2/26.
3849 *(new)* 1/30.
3860 *(ex8537)* 9/32.
1293 *(ex8271)* 3/34.
1557 *(ex8543)* 11/35.
1573 *(ex8541)* 12/36.
1575 *(ex8543)* 3/2/39.
3849 *(ex8548)* 11/10/41.
C1779 *(ex8539)* 15/5/43.
C1777 *(ex8552)* 19/8/44.
3855 *(ex8539)* 13/4/46.
23105 *(ex1503)* 27/7/51.

SHEDS:
Ipswich.
Kittybrewster 31/5/39.

RENUMBERED:
1563 19/5/46.
61563 17/4/48.

CONDEMNED:
10/4/53.

8564

Stratford.

To traffic 5/1920.

REPAIRS:
Str. 27/3-14/7/23.**G.**
Str. 28/11/24-5/5/25.**G.**
Str. 19/8/26-8/2/27.**G.**
Str. 9/27.**N/C.** *Vac.brake.*
Str. 27/4-7/7/28.**G.** *Coal guard on tender.*
Str. 30/11/29-3/2/30.**G.**
Str. 20/2-9/5/31.**G.**
Str. 4/9-11/11/32.**G.** *ACFI fitted.*
Str. 31/12/33-2/3/34.**G.**
Str. 11/5-19/7/35.**G.** *Reb to part 3.*
Str. 28/10-11/12/36.**G.**
Str. 29/8-17/9/37.**H.**
Str. 3-4/3/38.**L.**
Str. 6/11/38-26/1/39.**G.**
Str. 21/4-13/6/40.**G.**
Str. 21/1-28/3/42.**G.**
Str. 11/2-25/3/43.**L.**
Str. 19/9-13/11/43.**G.**
Str. 17/1-12/2/44.**L.**
Str. 15/4-18/5/45.**G.**
Str. 28/8-15/9/45.**L.**
Str. 17/5/46-24/1/47.**L.**
Str. 19/11-23/12/47.**G.**
Str. 10/12/48-15/1/49.**L.**
Str. 6/11-17/12/49.**G.**
Str. 14/2-22/3/50.**C/L.**
Str. 27/10-9/12/50.**C/L.**
Str. 24/1-1/3/52.**G.**
Str. 3-19/9/52.**C/L.**
Str. 7-25/4/53.**C/L.**
Str. 16/6-4/9/53.**C/L.**
Str. 20/12/54-29/1/55.**G.**
Str. 11/11/56-5/1/57.**G.**
Str. 16/9-3/10/57.**C/L.**

BOILERS:
1564.
1508 *(ex8522)* 8/2/27.
3837 *(new)* 7/7/28.
1561 *(ex8524)* 3/2/30.
1545 *(ex8577)* 11/11/32.
3834 *(ex8521)* 2/3/34.
4101 *(ex8516)* 19/7/35.
4137 *(new)* 11/12/36.
4132 *(ex8580)* 17/9/37.
4153 *(new)* 26/1/39.
4151 *(ex8515)* 13/6/40.
4152 *(ex8555)* 28/3/42.
4111 *(ex8573)* 13/11/43.
4120 *(ex8538)* 18/5/45.
4141 *(ex1519)* 23/12/47.
4113 *(ex1538)* 17/12/49.
Renumbered 27907 9/12/50.
27937 *(ex1574)* 1/3/52.
27953 *(new)* 29/1/55.

SHEDS:
Ipswich.
Stratford 19/3/27.
Ipswich 25/10/27.
Parkeston 26/6/32.
Ipswich 14/7/32.
Stratford 12/6/44.
Ipswich 20/8/44.

RENUMBERED:
1564 14/10/46.
61564 15/1/49.

CONDEMNED:
24/11/58.

WORKS CODES : Cow - Cowlairs, Dar - Darlington, Don - Doncaster, Ghd - Gateshead, Gor - Gorton, Inv - Inverurie, Str - Stratford.
REPAIR CODES : **C/H** - Casual Heavy, **C/L** - Casual Light, **G** - General, **H** - Heavy, **H/I** - Heavy Intermediate, **L** - Light, **L/I** - Light Intermediate, **N/C** - Not classified.

8560 had this number from June 1924 but still in 19in lettering on unlined grey paint. Approaching Witham East signal box it has the 6.50 a.m. stopping passenger train from Liverpool Street to Ipswich, consisting mainly of 6-wheeled coaches.

Based in 1925 at Norwich shed, 8510 is seen on the single line at West Runton with the Sheringham portion of an express to London (Liverpool Street).

The main line section of Liverpool Street station, taken in the early years of the grouping, showing 8558 leaving with a Norwich departure. Other engines include a 'Claud' 4-4-0 waiting to leave for Cambridge, a B17 and an N7.

'At the time of this photo - probably 1929 - 8515 was at Ipswich shed, and is seen here arriving at Beccles on a Yarmouth - London express of at least eleven bogie coaches.

8565

Stratford.

To traffic 5/1920.

REPAIRS:
Str. 9/11/23-8/3/24.**G.**
Str. 25/4-29/7/25.**G.**
Str. 22/7-27/11/26.**G.**
Str. 26/3-30/4/27.**H.**
Str. 23/2-12/5/28.**G.** *Vac.brake added.*
Str. 13/9-29/11/29.**G.** *Coal guard on tender.*
Str. 14/11/30-4/3/31.**G.**
Str. 24/4-30/6/33.**G.**
Str. 15/5-10/8/34.**G.**
Str. 24/9-9/11/35.**G.**
Str. 25/12/36-11/2/37.**G.** *R to pt 3.*
Str. 27/1-23/3/38.**G.**
Str. 12/2-11/4/40.**G.**
Str. 27/9-16/10/40.**L.**
Str. 23/9-8/11/41.**G.**
Str. 26/10-12/12/42.**G.**
Str. 8/2-2/4/43.**L.**
Str. 15/12/43-4/3/44.**G.**
Str. 2/12/45-5/1/46.**G.**
Str. 3/1-1/4/47.**G.**
Str. 9/1-14/3/49.**G.**
Str. 13-29/7/49.**C/L.**

Str. 10/10-23/11/51.**G.**
Str. 31/8-3/10/52.**C/L.**
Str. 20/8-2/10/54.**G.**

BOILERS:
1271.
1555 *(ex8555)* 30/4/27.
3831 *(ex8543)* 4/3/31.
1556 *(ex8568)* 30/6/33.
3852 *(ex8526)* 10/8/34.
3860 *(ex8522)* 9/11/35.
4142 *(new)* 11/2/37.
4112 *(ex8576)* 23/3/38.
4136 *(ex8569)* 11/4/40.
4134 *(ex8576)* 8/11/41.
4142 *(ex spare & 8545)* 12/12/42.
4102 *(ex8542)* 4/3/44.
4142 *(ex8557)* 5/1/46.
4135 *(ex1568)* 1/4/47.
4152 *(ex1512)* 14/3/49.
27921 *(ex1525)* 23/11/51.
27930 *(ex1579)* 2/10/54.

SHEDS:
Ipswich.
Cambridge 4/3/31.
March 28/3/31.
Ipswich 30/6/33.
Stratford 28/1/39.
Ipswich 13/3/39.
Stratford 24/5/44.

Grantham 7/12/49.
Peterborough 17/7/55.

RENUMBERED:
7479 12/12/42.
1565 22/9/46.
61565 12/3/49.

CONDEMNED:
1/1/57.

8566

Stratford.

To traffic 5/1920.

REPAIRS:
Str. 31/5-6/7/22.**L.**
Str. 29/2-3/7/24.**G.**
Str. 18/1-24/6/26.**G.**
Str. 8-28/10/26.**L.**
Str. 18/2-9/5/28.**G.** *Coal guard on tender. Vac.brake.*
Str. 24/9-26/11/29.**G.**
Str. 1/1-24/3/31.**G.**
Str. 13/10-18/12/31.**L.** *After collision.*
Str. 28/9-20/10/32.**H.**
Str. 6/4-9/6/33.**G.**

Str. 30/10-14/12/34.**G.**
Str. 13/4-30/5/36.**G.** *Reb to part 3.*
Str. 24/10-10/12/37.**G.**
Str. 12/3-19/5/39.**G.**
Str. 3/11/40-18/1/41.**G.**
Str. 18/4-19/6/43.**G.**
Str. 16/5-1/7/44.**G.**
Str. 25/2-17/3/45.**G.**
Str. 31/8-18/9/45.**L.**
Str. 9/9-28/10/46.**G.**
Str. 12/1-21/2/47.**L.**
Str. 5/3-1/5/48.**G.**
Str. 27/11/49-7/1/50.**G.**
Str. 26/3-16/6/50.**C/L.**
Str. 13/1-23/2/52.**G.**
Str. 31/1-12/3/54.**G.**
Str. 4/8-16/9/55.**C/L.**
Str. 23/9-27/10/55.**N/C.**
Str. 10/5-29/6/56.**G.**

BOILERS:
1565.
1556 *(ex8556)* 24/6/26.
1543 *(ex8551)* 26/11/29.
3821 *(ex8510)* 9/6/33.
3848 *(ex8545)* 14/12/34.
4111 *(ex8525)* 30/5/36.
4118 *(ex8550)* 10/12/37.
4116 *(ex8525)* 19/5/39.
4125 *(ex8519)* 18/1/41.
4134 *(ex8565)* 19/6/43.

WORKS CODES : Cow - Cowlairs, Dar - Darlington, Don - Doncaster, Ghd - Gateshead, Gor - Gorton, Inv - Inverurie, Str - Stratford.

REPAIR CODES : **C/H** - Casual Heavy, **C/L** - Casual Light, **G** - General, **H** - Heavy, **H/I** - Heavy Intermediate, **L** - Light, **L/I** - Light Intermediate, **N/C** - Not classified.

4162 *(ex8541)* 17/3/45.
4145 *(ex1575)* 28/10/46.
4126 *(ex1527)* 1/5/48.
4125 *(ex1570)* 7/1/50.
27934 *(ex1570)* 23/2/52.
27908 *(ex1574)* 12/3/54.
27942 *(ex1535)* 29/6/56.

SHEDS:
Ipswich.
Yarmouth 24/3/25.
Norwich 20/10/34.
Yarmouth 1/6/35.
Norwich 12/4/36.
Yarmouth 20/3/38.
Norwich 10/7/38.
Yarmouth 25/9/38.
Norwich 12/3/39.
Yarmouth 6/8/39.
Norwich 19/5/40.
Yarmouth 4/5/41.
Ipswich 15/10/44.
Norwich 1/6/58.

RENUMBERED:
1566 2/10/46.
61566 24/4/48.

CONDEMNED:
26/1/59.

8567

Stratford.

To traffic 6/1920.

REPAIRS:
Str. 31/12/23-24/4/24.**G.**
Str. 18/5-26/8/25.**G.** *Diamond tube cleaner.*
Str. 18/3-13/7/27.**G.** *Tube cleaner removed.*
Str. 6/12/28-22/3/29.**G.** Coal guard on tender.
Str. 3/7-17/10/30.**G.**
Str. 22/10-13/11/30.**L.**
Str. 25/11/31-2/4/32.**G.** *ACFI fitted.*

Str. 18/5-19/7/33.**G.**
Str. 1/2-4/4/35.**G.** *Rebuilt to part 3.*
Str. 15/11/36-9/1/37.**G.**
Str. 3-14/9/37.**H.**
Str. 16/3-28/4/38.**G.**
Str. 10/9-27/10/39.**G.**
Str. 21/10-14/11/40.**L.**
Str. 3/9-17/10/41.**G.**
Str. 22/10-24/12/43.**G.**
Str. 13-14/4/44.**N/C.** *Ambulance valve.*
Str. 12-19/3/45.**G.**
Str. 19-30/4/45.**L.**
Str. 28/10-24/11/45.**G.**
Str. 14-21/9/46.**L.**
Str. 27/2-9/4/47.**G.**
Str. 28/12/47-17/3/48.**G.** *Bow Junc.accident.*
Str. 1/1-4/2/50.**G.**
Str. 29/1-21/3/52.**G.**
Str. 29/1-24/2/54.**N/C.**
Str. 27/9-6/11/54.**G.**
Str. 20/6-4/8/56.**C/L.**

BOILERS:
1273.
1540 *(ex1517)* 26/8/25.
1544 *(ex8548)* 13/7/27.
3845 *(new)* 22/3/29.
1560 *(ex8508)* 2/4/32.
3831 *(ex8565)* 19/7/33.
4116 *(new)* 4/4/35.
4140 *(new)* 9/1/37.
4133 *(ex8527)* 14/9/37.
4141 *(ex8522)* 28/4/38.
4115 *(ex8517)* 27/10/39.
4155 *(ex8520)* 17/10/41.
4131 *(ex8527)* 24/12/43.
4136 *(ex8550)* 19/3/45.
4128 *(ex8522)* 24/11/45.
4107 *(ex1571)* 9/4/47.
4120 *(ex1564)* 17/3/48.
4119 *(ex1557)* 4/2/50.
27938 *(ex1515)* 21/3/52.
27951 *(new)* 6/11/54.

SHEDS:
Norwich.
Ipswich 17/3/26.
Norwich 15/4/26.

Parkeston 30/10/26.
Colchester 14/4/31.
Stratford 25/9/39.
Colchester 8/9/40.
Stratford 28/12/40.
Colchester 20/5/51.
Stratford 11/11/51.
Grantham 1/2/53.
Peterborough 9/9/56.
Cambridge 24/2/57.
Bury St Edmunds 24/3/57.

RENUMBERED:
1567 27/10/46.
E1567 13/3/48.
61567 4/2/50.

CONDEMNED:
11/11/58.

8568

Stratford.

To traffic 6/1920.

REPAIRS:
Str. 8/12/23-10/4/24.**G.**
Str. 15/1-4/6/26.**G.**
Str. 10/11/27-25/2/28.**G.** *Coal guard on tender.*
Str. 16/11/29-14/2/30.**G.**
Str. 22/8-31/10/31.**G.** *ACFI fitted.*
Str. 23/3-29/5/33.**G.**
Str. 3/5-5/7/35.**G.**
Str. 14/1-12/3/37.**G.**
Str. 19-25/3/38.**L.**
Str. 4/12/38-17/2/39.**G.**
Str. 28/12/39-3/1/40.**L.**
Str. 6/2-30/4/41.**G.** *Reb to part 3.*
Str. 15/9-31/10/42.**G.**
Str. 10/9-14/10/44.**G.**
Str. 16/4-14/5/45.**L.**
Str. 26/11-29/12/45.**L.**
Str. 27/10-10/12/46.**G.**
Str. 29/8-12/10/48.**G.**
Str. 27-29/9/49.**C/L.**
Str. 22/6-16/8/50.**G.**

Str. 15-21/2/52.**N/C.** *Tablet exch.app.fitted.*
Str. 29/10-13/12/52.**G.**
Str. 15/3-18/6/55.**G.**
Str. 6/12/57-25/1/58.**G.**
Str. 29/7/59.*Not repaired.*

BOILERS:
1272.
3802 *(ex1569)* 10/4/24.
3803 *(ex8552)* 4/6/26.
1556 *(ex8566)* 14/2/30.
1577 *(ex8539)* 29/5/33.
1571 *(ex8570)* 5/7/35.
1549 *(ex8570)* 12/3/37.
1579 *(ex8552)* 17/2/39.
4160 *(new)* 30/4/41.
4146 *(ex8561)* 31/10/42.
4135 *(ex spare & 8540)* 14/10/44.
4153 *(ex8544)* 10/12/46.
4145 *(ex1566)* 12/10/48.
4129 *(ex1561)* 16/8/50.
Renumbered 27939 21/2/52.
27948 *(ex1520)* 13/12/52.
27906 *(ex1549)* 18/6/55.
27939 *(ex1541)* 25/1/58.

SHEDS:
Norwich.
Cambridge 14/6/24.
March 30/10/24.
Parkeston 12/10/26.
Stratford 13/7/35.
Parkeston 1/11/35.
Stratford 21/8/38.
Norwich 27/5/43.
Yarmouth 4/2/45.
Norwich 16/1/46.
Stratford 5/5/46.
Colchester 19/4/47.
Stratford 7/6/47.
Ipswich 13/5/51.
Norwich 1/7/51.
Yarmouth Beach 28/6/53.
Yarmouth 20/9/53.
Ipswich 17/1/54.
Yarmouth Beach 25/4/54.
Ipswich 4/7/54.
Norwich 15/8/54.

RENUMBERED:
7482 31/10/42.
1568 13/9/46.
61568 9/10/48.

CONDEMNED:
3/8/59.

8519 was one of the six which Stratford rebuilt with Lentz valves and is seen climbing Brentwood bank with a down express from London to Ipswich, its home station.

8511 heading south between Cambridge and Trumpington with an empty stock train. The LNWR signal and cabin on the left mark where the line to Bedford, Bletchley and Oxford diverged.

This is the 'Antwerp Continental' boat train climbing Brentwood bank on its journey from Liverpool Street to Harwich (Parkeston Quay) with 8533 in charge. Before they lost the boat train workings to B17, the B12s put on record some amazing performances on these tightly timed, and heavily loaded trains.

Trains leaving Liverpool Street station were faced with the disadvantage of the severe Bethnal Green incline which started a short distance from the platform end. In this view 8547 of Stratford attacks the incline with a Cambridge service.

8569

Stratford.

To traffic 6/1920.

REPAIRS:
Str. 4/10/23-23/2/24.**G.**
Str. 5/5-4/9/25.**G.**
Str. 9/3-13/7/27.**G.**
Str. 21/11-4/12/28.**N/C.** *Vac.brake added.*
Str. 19/1-16/5/29.**G.** *Coal guard on tender.*
Str. 5/6-9/9/30.**G.**
Str. 2-29/7/31.**G.**
Str. 4/3-20/5/32.**G.** *ACFI fitted.*
Str. 2/10-8/12/33.**G.** *Reb to part 3.*
Str. 8/4-31/5/35.**G.**
Str. 9/11-24/12/36.**G.**
Str. 11/4-26/5/38.**G.**
Str. 4/12/39-26/1/40.**G.**
Str. 3/1-28/2/41.**L.**
Str. 24/5-3/7/42.**G.**
Str. 5/3-29/5/43.**G.**
Str. 6/8-9/9/44.**G.**
Str. 4/7-10/8/45.**L.**
Str. 22/1-5/3/46.**G.**

Str. 12/11/47-7/1/48.**G.**
Str. 17/4-28/5/49.**G.**
Str. 7/9-26/10/50.**G.**
Str. 24/4-4/5/51.**C/L.**
Str. 25/3-7/4/52.**C/L.**
Str. 1/12/52-24/1/53.**G.**
Str. 20/2-7/5/55.**G.**

BOILERS:
3802.
1544 *(ex1544)* 23/2/24.
1518 *(ex1544)* 4/9/25.
3847 *(new)* 16/5/29.
1551 *(ex8527)* 20/5/32.
4109 *(new)* 8/12/33.
4113 *(ex8517)* 31/5/35.
4139 *(new)* 24/12/36.
4136 *(ex8545)* 26/5/38.
4138 *(ex8545)* 26/1/40.
4150 *(ex8557)* 3/7/42.
4124 *(ex8535)* 9/9/44.
4125 *(ex8519)* 5/3/46.
4133 *(ex1557)* 7/1/48.
4162 *(ex1516)* 28/5/49.
27904 *(ex1520)* 26/10/50.
27909 *(ex1546)* 24/1/53.
27916 *(ex1523)* 7/5/55.

SHEDS:
Norwich.
Yarmouth 11/3/38.
Norwich 3/4/38.
Yarmouth 13/11/38.
Norwich 3/9/39.
Yarmouth 24/11/40.
Norwich 6/7/41.
Yarmouth 24/7/41.
Norwich 24/8/41.
Yarmouth 18/3/42.
Ipswich 1/10/44.
Yarmouth 21/10/45.
Ipswich 24/8/47.

RENUMBERED:
1569 17/11/46.
61569 28/5/49.

CONDEMNED:
1/1/57.

8570

Stratford.

To traffic 6/1920.

REPAIRS:
Str. 1/10/23-24/1/24.**G.**
Str. 16/9-11/10/24.**L.**
Str. 24/6-2/10/25.**G.**
Str. 26/4-25/7/27.**G.**
Str. 5/12/28-22/3/29.**G.** *Vac.brake. Coal guard on tender.*
Str. 24/4-4/7/30.**G.** *Ross 'Pops' fitted.*
Str. 10/1-10/2/31.**L.**
Str. 15/1-29/4/32. **G.** *ACFI fitted.*
Str. 19/9-21/11/33.**G.**
Str. 16/2-11/4/35.**G.**
Str. 24/11/36-21/1/37.**G.**
Str. 18/9-8/10/37.**L.**
Str. 17/11/38-18/3/39.**G.**
Str. 27/4-20/6/41.**G.** *ACFI removed.*
Str. 24/7-6/8/41.**L.**
Str. 15/8-6/11/43.**G.** *Reb to part 3.*
Str. 25/2-14/4/45.**G.**
Str. 21/5-1/7/46.**G.**
Str. 22/7-9/9/46.**L.** *Collision damage.*
Str. 22/2-16/4/48.**G.**
Str. 20/6-23/7/49.**C/L.**
Str. 16/10-21/11/49.**G.**
Str. 28/10-15/12/51.**G.**

WORKS CODES : Cow - Cowlairs, Dar - Darlington, Don - Doncaster, Ghd - Gateshead, Gor - Gorton, Inv - Inverurie, Str - Stratford.
REPAIR CODES : **C/H** - Casual Heavy, **C/L** - Casual Light, **G** - General, **H** - Heavy, **H/I** - Heavy Intermediate, **L** - Light, **L/I** - Light Intermediate, **N/C** - Not classified.

79

In LNER days 8552 heads east through Romford with a London - Southend service...

...and more than a quarter of a century later 61578 runs into Southend (Victoria) with a train from Liverpool Street on, 31 July 1954. PhotographGresley Society.

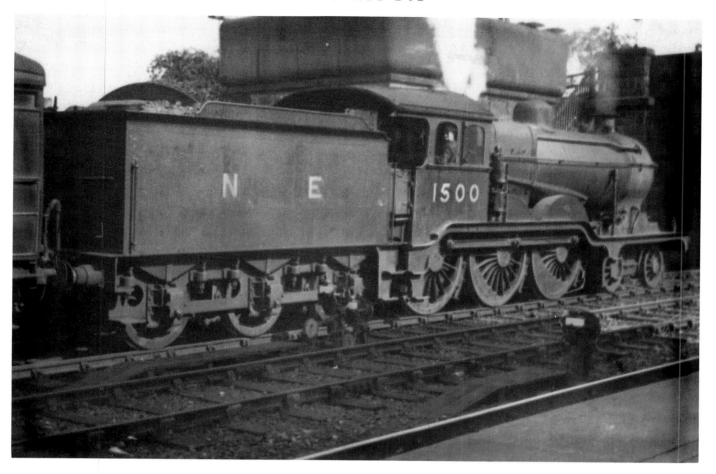

The class leader, in austere colours, stands at Inverurie with a G.N.o S service.

8552 runs into Aberdeen with a G.N.o.S. service, 1946.

Str. 25/9-7/11/53.**G.**
Str. 22/6-29/7/54.**C/L.**
Str. 30/9-11/10/54.**C/L.**
Str. 18/3-12/5/55.**C/L.**
Str. 14/3-3/5/56.**G.**

BOILERS:
3803.
1562 *(ex1562)* 24/1/24.
1537 *(ex8535)* 25/7/27.
1547 *(ex1502)* 22/3/29.
3853 *(new)* 4/7/30.
1553 *(ex8518)* 29/4/32.
1571 *(ex8574)* 21/11/33.
1549 *(ex8544)* 11/4/35.
3820 *(ex8513)* 21/1/37.
1549 *(ex8568)* 18/3/39.
3832 *(ex8276)* 20/6/41.
4129 *(ex8571)* 6/11/43.
4156 *(ex8527)* 14/4/45.
4122 *(ex8520)* 1/7/46.
4125 *(ex1569)* 16/4/48.
4123 *(ex1547)* 21/11/49.
27900 *(ex1516)* 15/12/51.
27927 *(ex1562)* 7/11/53.
27926 *(ex1556)* 3/5/56.

SHEDS:
Norwich.
Yarmouth 30/12/33.
Norwich 29/11/36.
Yarmouth 31/3/37.
Norwich 19/9/37.
Yarmouth 19/10/37.
Norwich 13/11/38.
Yarmouth 26/3/39.
Norwich 19/5/40.
Yarmouth 24/11/40.
Norwich 18/3/42.
Ipswich 26/12/43.

RENUMBERED:
1570 26/6/46.
61570 10/4/48.

CONDEMNED:
31/3/58.

8571

Beyer Peacock 6487.

To traffic 22/8/28.

REPAIRS:
Str. 25/10-19/11/28.**L.**
Str. 5/4-21/7/30.**G.**
Str. 10/10-24/12/31.**G.** *Reb to pt 1.*
Str. 30/3-6/7/33.**G.** *Reb to part 3.*
Str. 19/1-14/3/35.**G.**
Str. 24/2-8/4/36.**G.**
Str. 23/5-16/7/37.**G.**
Str. 26/3-13/4/38.**L.**
Str. 29/11/38-2/3/39.**G.**
Str. 16/8-1/11/40.**G.**
Str. 24/1-19/3/43.**G.**
Str. 20/11-1/12/43.**L.**
Str. 13/4/44.**N/C.** *Ambulance valve.*
Str. 18/10-25/11/44.**G.**
Str. 8/2-10/3/45.**L.**
Str. 13/11-22/12/45.**L.**
Str. 9/10-6/12/46.**G.**
Str. 5/9-19/10/48.**G.**
Str. 21/5-24/6/50.**G.**
Str. 28/4-30/5/52.**G.**
Str. 17/2-9/4/54.**G.**
Str. 7/11/55-13/1/56.**C/L.**
Str. 9/12/56-26/1/57.**G.**

Str. 25/7-2/8/57.**C/L.**

BOILERS:
1571.
3856 *(ex8529)* 24/12/31.
4105 *(new)* 6/7/33.
4108 *(ex8575)* 8/4/36.
4101 *(ex8564)* 16/7/37.
4145 *(ex8538)* 2/3/39.
4129 *(ex8512)* 1/11/40.
4157 *(ex8574)* 19/3/43.
4107 *(ex8578)* 25/11/44.
4148 *(ex8542)* 6/12/46.
4146 *(ex1573)* 19/10/48.
4121 *(ex1574)* 24/6/50.
27943 *(ex1561)* 30/5/52.
27929 *(ex1572)* 9/4/54.
27907 *(ex1546)* 26/1/57.

SHEDS:
Gorton 6/6/28.
Stratford 14/9/28.
Colchester 3/12/39.
Stratford 8/9/40.
Colchester 28/12/40.
Stratford 2/1/43.
Grantham 1/2/53.
Ipswich 15/3/53.
Norwich 17/11/57.

RENUMBERED:
1571 14/6/46.
61571 16/10/48.

CONDEMNED:
31/12/59.

8572

Beyer Peacock 6488.

To traffic 24/8/28.

REPAIRS:
Str. 25/5-22/6/29.**L.**
Str. 3/5-14/8/30.**G.**
Str. 26/11/31-24/3/32.**G.** *R to pt 1.*
Str. 17/10-22/12/33.**G.** *R to pt 3.*
Str. 28/2-25/4/35.**G.**
Str. 15/4-9/6/36.**G.**
Str. 15/3-23/4/38.**G.**
Str. 2-10/2/39.**L.**
Str. 18/9-1/11/39.**G.**
Str. 17/7-12/9/41.**G.**
Str. 12/9-6/11/43.**G.**
Str. 7-14/3/44.**L.**
Str. 24/6-18/8/45.**G.**
Str. 22/9-21/11/46.**G.**
Str. 4/4-9/5/48.**G.**
Str. 25/9-22/10/49.**G.**
Str. 31/10-2/11/49.**N/C.**
Str. 4/9-11/10/51.**G.**
Str. 17-23/7/52.**C/L.**
Str. 15/12/52-3/1/53.**C/L.**
Str. 22/3-24/4/53.**N/C.**
Str. 28/10-5/12/53.**G.**
Str. 16-24/9/54.**C/L.**
Str. 18/12/55-3/2/56.**G.**
Str. 27/12/57-14/2/58.**G.**

BOILERS:
1572.
1575 *(ex8575)* 24/3/32.
4110 *(new)* 22/12/33.
4104 *(ex8580)* 9/6/36.
4142 *(ex8565)* 23/4/38.
4108 *(ex8509)* 1/11/39.

1550 leaving the loop at Trumpington on 18 October 1924 with an up goods for London, the engine working back to its home shed of Stratford. Despite being ex-works 30th June 1923 from a general repair its only change was the substitution of the smaller LNER number plate for the large brass G.E. type of the same number. Photograph H.G.Household.

4149 *(ex8525)* 12/9/41.
4116 *(ex8546)* 6/11/43.
4132 *(ex8559)* 18/8/45.
4155 *(ex8509)* 21/11/46.
4122 *(ex1570)* 9/5/48.
4157 *(ex1533)* 22/10/49.
27929 *(ex1519)* 11/10/51.
27933 *(ex1542)* 5/12/53.
27922 *(ex1519)* 3/2/56.
27950 *(ex1557)* 14/2/58.

SHEDS:
Gorton 13/6/28.
Stratford 14/9/28.
Parkeston 26/3/39.
Stratford 25/9/39.
Colchester 3/12/39.
Stratford 18/10/43.
Colchester 8/1/44.
Stratford 11/11/44.
Grantham 1/2/53.
Ipswich 15/3/53.
Norwich 11/10/59.

RENUMBERED:
1572 16/6/46.
61572 1/5/48.

CONDEMNED:
20/9/61.

In the early 1930s, the increasing number of B17 class relegated the B12s on to more mundane duties such as this goods working which is seen with 8560 in charge.

8577 of Ipswich, one of the part 2 engines equipped with Lentz valves, leaving Worksop with the Harwich - Manchester boat train.

8573

Beyer Peacock 6489.

To traffic 27/8/28.

REPAIRS:
Str. 25/10-17/11/28.**L.**
Str. 14-31/10/29.**L.**
Str. 14/3-13/6/30.**G.**
Str. 26/9-14/12/31.**G.** *Reb to pt 1.*
Str. 25/4-14/7/33.**G.** *Reb to pt 3.*
Str. 3/1-20/2/35.**G.**
Str. 16/3-8/5/36.**G.**
Str. 11/10-19/11/37.**G.**
Str. 23/2-3/3/38.**L.**
Str. 19/3-2/6/39.**G.**
Str. 15/2-11/4/41.**G.**
Str. 20/6-17/9/43.**G.**
Str. 21-23/2/44.**N/C.**
Str. 12/11-16/12/44.**G.**
Str. 10-26/5/45.**N/C.**
Str. 1/6-11/8/45.**L.**
Str. 3/11-20/12/46.**G.**
Str. 30/3-7/5/48.**G.** *Cont.blow down fitted.*
Str. 26/7-10/8/48.**L.**
Str. 6/11-16/12/49.**G.**
Str. 8-24/1/51.**C/L.**
Str. 21/11-22/12/51.**G.**
Str. 24-29/12/51.**N/C.**
Str. 12/9-4/10/52.**C/L.**
Str. 23/3-10/4/53.**C/L.**
Str. 26/6-21/8/53.**G.**
Str. 3/10-26/11/55.**G.**
Str. 18/11-21/12/57.**G.**

BOILERS:
1573.

3855 *(ex8513)* 14/12/31.
4107 *(new)* 14/7/33.
4137 *(ex8564)* 19/11/37.
4117 *(ex8514)* 2/6/39.
4111 *(ex8577)* 11/4/41.
4143 *(ex8517)* 17/9/43.
4130 *(ex8544)* 16/12/44.
4146 *(ex7482)* 20/12/46.
4158 *(ex1546)* 7/5/48.
4131 *(ex1510)* 16/12/49.
Renumbered 27913 24/1/51.
27932 *(ex1557)* 22/12/51.
27901 *(ex1545)* 21/8/53.
27912 *(ex1577)* 26/11/55.
27903 *(ex1516)* 21/12/57.

SHEDS:
Gorton.
Stratford 14/9/28.
Parkeston 26/3/39.
Stratford 25/9/39.
Colchester 3/12/39.
Stratford 15/2/41.
Colchester 13/4/41.
Stratford 11/11/44.
Cambridge 17/2/57.

RENUMBERED:
1573 12/5/46.
61573 7/8/48.

CONDEMNED:
1/1/59.

8574

Beyer Peacock 6490.

To traffic 29/8/28.

REPAIRS:
Str. 14/6-10/7/29.**L.**
Str. 19/4-16/7/30.**G.**
Str. 20/10/31-6/1/32.**G.** *Reb to pt 1.*
Str. 7/5-19/7/33.**G.** *Reb to part 3.*
Str. 31/12/34-15/2/35.**G.**
Str. 8/3-1/5/36.**G.**
Str. 19/4-24/6/37.**G.**
Str. 26/2-2/3/38.**L.**
Str. 19-20/5/38.**L.**
Str. 7/11/38-9/2/39.**G.**
Str. 4/12/40-17/1/41.**G.**
Str. 5/12/42-23/1/43.**G.**
Str. 27/2-22/4/44.**G.**
Str. 12/5-9/6/45.**L.**
Str. 17/1-26/2/46.**G.**
Str. 19-28/3/46.**L.**
Str. 22/2-27/3/48.**G.**
Str. 29/10-3/12/49.**G.**
Str. 17/12/51-2/2/52.**G.**
Str. 12/1-5/3/54.**G.**
Str. 2/11/54-29/1/55.**C/L.**

BOILERS:
1574.
1571 *(ex8571)* 6/1/32.
4106 *(new)* 19/7/33.
4123 *(ex8518)* 1/5/36.
4120 *(ex8542)* 24/6/37.
4110 *(ex8557)* 9/2/39.
4157 *(new)* 17/1/41.
4138 *(ex8569)* 23/1/43.
4154 *(ex8555)* 22/4/44.
4114 *(ex8555)* 26/2/46.
4121 *(ex1542)* 27/3/48.
4160 *(ex1519)* 3/12/49.
27908 *(ex1541)* 2/2/52.

27915 *(ex1540)* 5/3/54.

SHEDS:
Gorton.
Stratford 20/9/28.
Parkeston 21/8/38.
Stratford 25/9/39.
Colchester 3/12/39.
Stratford 15/2/42.
Colchester 11/7/42.
Stratford 2/1/43.
Colchester 16/1/43.
Ipswich 12/6/44.
Stratford 20/8/44.
Grantham 1/2/53.

RENUMBERED:
7488 23/1/43.
1574 3/11/46.
61574 27/3/48.

CONDEMNED:
1/1/57.

8575

Beyer Peacock 6491.

To traffic 14/9/28.

REPAIRS:
Str. 14-28/11/28.**L.**
Str. 17/5-29/8/30.**G.**
Str. 21/11/31-26/2/32.**G.** *R to pt 1.*
Str. 26/9-24/11/33.**G.** *Reb to pt 3.*
Str. 22/1-8/3/35.**G.**
Str. 13/2-25/3/36.**G.**
Str. 8/4-11/6/37.**G.**

8560 makes a third appearance, this time in summer 1939 and on distinctly strange ground. Transferred to Scotland in March that year it was then loaned to Eastfield shed to work the Glasgow - Oban summer excursions, for which the 12-coach green and cream painted sets of open tourist stock were used. The assisting engine is 9695, the only one of class D36. At Cowlairs West Junc. the train diverges onto the suburban line through Alexandra Parade and Duke Street stations to pick up its passengers in Queen Street Low Level.

As one of the B12 class sent to the Northern Scottish Area, 8539 went from Ipswich to Kittybrewster in June 1933 and remained working in that area until its withdrawal in November 1954, when it was the last example fitted with a Belpaire firebox. It is seen here at Craigellachie on April 11th 1946 at the head of a fast train to Aberdeen. Photograph H.C.Casserley.

Str. 24/2-1/3/38.**L.**
Str. 4-22/7/38.**L.**
Str. 12/1-31/3/39.**G.**
Str. 28/12/40-20/2/41.**G.**
Str. 10/1-6/3/43.**G.**
Str. 14-23/10/43.**L.**
Str. 28-29/3/44.**N/C.** *Ambulance valve.*
Str. 17/1-10/3/45.**G.**
Str. 14/10-8/11/45.**L.**
Str. 25/6-20/8/46.**G.**
Str. 3/3-21/4/48.**G.**
Str. 14-29/10/49.**C/L.**
Str. 7/5-3/6/50.**G.**
Str. 21/3-7/4/51.**C/L.**
Str. 26/5-22/7/52.**G.**
Str. 8/4-4/6/54.**G.**
Str. 19/8-3/9/54.**C/L.**
Str. 20/12/55-11/2/56.**G.**
Str. 20-28/2/56.**N/C.**
Str. 25/11-28/12/57.**G.**
Str. 13-20/1/58.**N/C.**

BOILERS:
1575.
1557 *(ex8539)* 26/2/32.
4108 *(new)* 24/11/33.
4122 *(ex8542)* 25/3/36.
4124 *(ex8578)* 11/6/37.
4147 *(ex8547)* 31/3/39.
4137 *(ex8517)* 20/2/41.
4109 *(ex8538)* 6/3/43.
4145 *(ex7491)* 10/3/45.
4151 *(ex7426)* 20/8/46.

4124 *(ex1520)* 21/4/48.
4127 *(ex1558)* 3/6/50.
Renumbered 27916 7/4/51.
27945 *(ex1571)* 22/7/52.
27914 *(ex1537)* 11/2/56.
27916 *(ex1569)* 28/12/57.

SHEDS:
Gorton.
Stratford 6/6/29.
Parkeston 21/8/38.
Stratford 25/9/39.
Colchester 3/12/39.
Stratford 13/4/41.
Colchester 12/12/42.
Stratford 11/11/44.
Cambridge 6/1/37.
Kings Lynn 7/4/57.
Cambridge 24/11/57.

RENUMBERED:
1575 22/6/46.
61575 10/4/48.

CONDEMNED:
6/4/59.

8576

Beyer Peacock 6492.

To traffic 31/8/28.

REPAIRS:
Str. 30/11/28-3/5/29.**L.**
Str. 22/11/30-11/2/31.**G.**
Str. 2/6-22/8/32.**G.** *Reb to part 3.*
Str. 17/12/32-9/1/33.**L.**
Str. 1-6/3/33.**L.**
Str. 27/11/33-26/1/34.**G.**
Str. 26/3-23/5/35.**G.**
Str. 16/10-3/12/36.**G.**
Str. 1/1-11/2/38.**G.**
Str. 23/5-3/8/39.**G.**
Str. 5/3-23/4/41.**G.**
Str. 27/9-1/10/42.**L.**
Str. 18/7-6/10/43.**G.**
Str. 4-6/4/44.**N/C.** *Ambulance valve.*
Str. 13/2-7/3/45.**L.**
Str. 16/9-13/10/45.**G.** *Cont.blow down fitted.*
Str. 19/2-31/3/47.**G.**
Str. 8/4-19/5/48.**L.**
Str. 4/11-14/12/48.**G.**
Str. 5/9-14/10/50.**G.**
Str. 25/6-16/8/52.**G.**
Str. 12/3-15/4/53.**N/C.**
Str. 28/7-11/9/54.**G.**
Str. 20/7-15/9/56.**G.**

BOILERS:
1576.
4101 *(new)* 22/8/32.
4109 *(ex8569)* 23/5/35.
4112 *(ex8577)* 3/12/36.
4114 *(ex8516)* 11/2/38.

4134 *(ex8546)* 3/8/39.
4148 *(ex8559)* 23/4/41.
4103 *(ex8537)* 6/10/43.
4101 *(ex8537)* 13/10/45.
4144 *(ex1523)* 31/3/47.
4118 *(ex spare & 1544)* 14/12/48.
27903 *(ex1514)* 14/10/50.
27913 *(ex1573)* 16/8/52.
27931 *(ex1557)* 11/9/54.
27923 *(ex1533)* 15/9/56.

SHEDS:
Gorton.
Stratford 20/9/28.
Colchester 21/5/29.
Ipswich 14/2/31.
Colchester 15/2/34.
Stratford 8/1/39.
Colchester 26/3/39.
Stratford 20/10/45.
Colchester 7/12/46.
Stratford 8/2/47.
Cambridge 6/1/57.

RENUMBERED:
1576 2/3/46.
61576 11/12/48.

CONDEMNED:
1/1/59.

WORKS CODES : Cow - Cowlairs, Dar - Darlington, Don - Doncaster, Ghd - Gateshead, Gor - Gorton, Inv - Inverurie, Str - Stratford.
REPAIR CODES : **C/H** - Casual Heavy, **C/L** - Casual Light, **G** - General, **H** - Heavy, **H/I** - Heavy Intermediate, **L** - Light, **L/I** - Light Intermediate, **N/C** - Not classified.

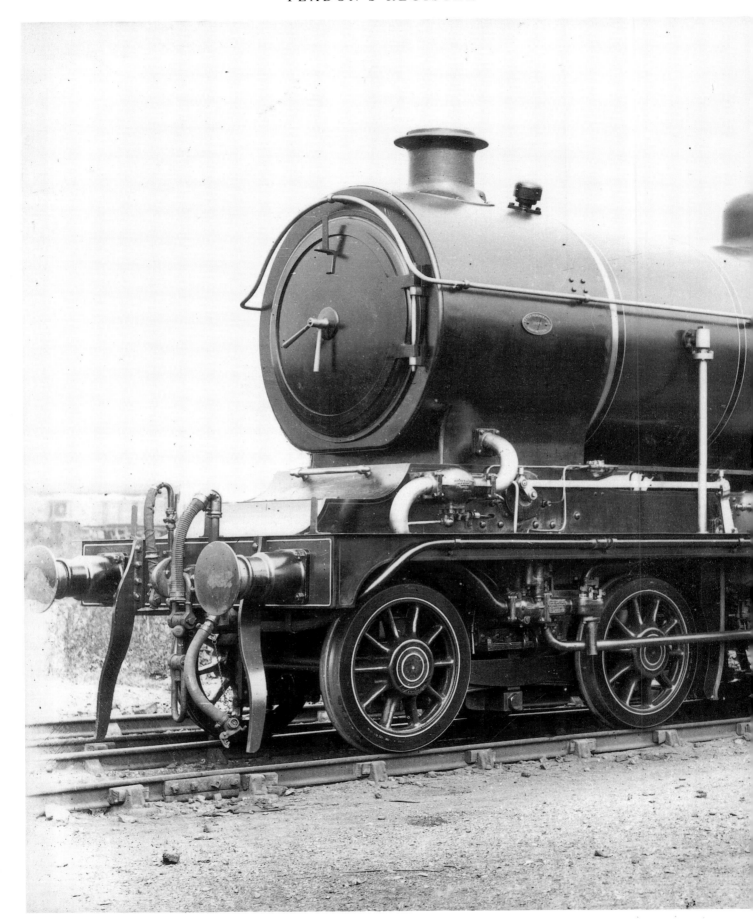

8571 as originally turned out by Beyer Peacock in August 1928 and photographed at Stratford where it arrived, after three months running-in at Gorton, the following month. Lacking decorative valances and sporting conventional safety valves, the engine presented something of an austere appearance at Stratford although it remained on the Great Eastern for its entire life apart from a very brief exile to Grantham for a six weeks in early 1953. It survived until New Years Eve 1959.

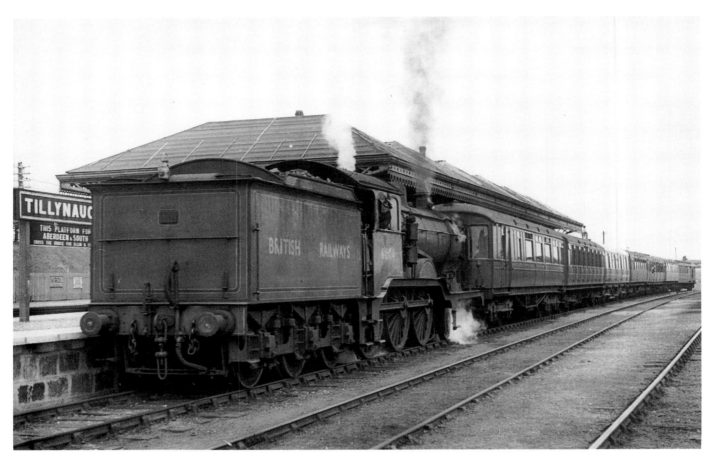

61504 is about to leave Tillynaught for Keith with this all-stations train during 1949. In spite of two subsequent renumberings, its tender still has the 8504 LNER number plate which Stratford attached in September 1924. The interesting mixture of coaches seen will be noted.

Much more typical of the work done by the class in the far north is this express fish train which is seen approaching Kittybrewster in 1947 behind 1563 and 1543, the engines appearing in black and green liveries respectively. The train worked through to London, being re-engined at Aberdeen by an LNER pacific or V2 2-6-2.

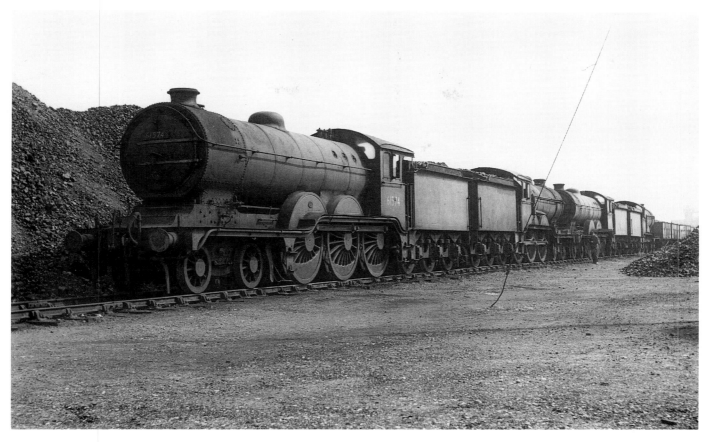

The electrification of the line to Southend-on-Sea was responsible for this melancholy sight, the four B12/3s, 61574, 61541, 61565 and 61557 being withdrawn from stock on January 1st 1957. It is not known if there was reluctance to cut them up, or whether they were prudently just being kept handy against any electric teething troubles, but the date of this photograph was May 12th 1957. Photograph A.R.Goult.

8577

Beyer Peacock 6493.

To traffic 12/9/28.

REPAIRS:
Str. 14-30/11/28.**L.**
Str. 25/11/29-26/2/30.**G.** *Indicator gear fitted.*
Str. 24/8-6/11/31.**G.** *Rebuilt to part 1.ACFI fitted.*
Str. 5/9-7/11/32.**G.**
Str. 14/11/33-12/1/34.**G.** *R to pt 3.*
Str. 6/2-22/3/35.**G.**
Str. 29/4-3/7/36.**G.**
Str. 17/10-2/12/37.**G.**
Str. 8/5-1/7/39.**G.**
Str. 17/12/40-22/2/41.**G.**
Str. 17/8-31/10/42.**G.**
Str. 31/7-9/8/43.**L.**
Str. 26/2-15/4/44.**G.**
Str. 22/3-6/4/45.**L.**
Str. 31/7-25/8/45.**L.**
Str. 14/10-20/11/45.**G.**
Str. 14/6-16/10/46.**L.** *New cyls.*
Str. 30/11-30/12/46.**L.**
Str. 17/5-4/7/47.**G.**
Str. 9/1-7/3/49.**G.**
Str. 6/11-9/12/49.**C/L.**

Str. 5-12/5/50.**C/L.**
Str. 3-19/8/50.**C/L.**
Str. 7-15/9/50.**C/L.**
Str. 13/4-2/6/51.**H/I.**
Str. 4-15/9/51.**C/L.**
Str. 17/1-12/3/53.**G.**
Str. 7/8-23/9/55.**G.**
Str. 3-12/10/55.**N/C.**
Str. 14/7-31/8/57.**G.**
Str. 23/9/59 *Not repaired.*

BOILERS:
1577.
1545 *(ex8524)* 6/11/31.
1578 *(ex8578)* 7/11/32.
4112 *(new)* 12/1/34.
4117 *(ex8519)* 3/7/36.
4122 *(ex8575)* 2/12/37.
4111 *(ex8522)* 1/7/39.
4130 *(ex8550)* 22/2/41.
4145 *(ex8519)* 31/10/42.
4117 *(ex8525)* 15/4/44.
4150 *(ex spare & 8569)* 25/8/45.
4109 *(ex1554)* 4/7/47.
4144 *(ex1576)* 7/3/49.
Renumbered 27920 2/6/51.
27912 *(ex1554)* 12/3/53.
27946 *(ex1512)* 23/9/55.
27929 *(ex1571)* 31/8/57.

SHEDS:
Gorton.
Stratford 3/10/28.
Ipswich 18/12/28.
Stratford 26/2/30.
Ipswich 4/4/30.
Stratford 31/5/44.
Ipswich 14/10/44.
Norwich 3/8/58.
Cambridge 12/4/59.

RENUMBERED:
7491 31/10/42.
1577 9/10/46.
61577 5/3/49.

CONDEMNED:
28/9/59.

8578

Beyer Peacock 6494.

To traffic 21/9/28.

REPAIRS:
Str. 21/1-9/5/29.**L.**
Str. 10/7-3/10/30.**G.**
Str. 16/1-17/4/31.**G.** *After collision at Thorpe-Le-Soken. Tender No.20*

fitted.
Str. 28/7-27/10/32.**G.** *Reb to pt 3.*
Str. 25/1-15/3/34.**G.**
Str. 26/10-7/12/34.**H.**
Str. 23/10-31/12/35.**G.**
Str. 21/3-14/5/37.**G.**
Str. 21-28/6/38.**L.**
Str. 12/9-2/11/38.**G.**
Str. 19/3-10/5/40.**G.**
Str. 12/2-7/4/42.**G.**
Str. 22-26/2/44.**N/C.**
Str. 4/7-17/8/44.**G.**
Str. 31/3-14/5/46.**G.**
Str. 15/3-13/5/47.**G.**
Str. 28/1-8/3/48.**L.**
Str. 22/4-1/6/48.**L.**
Str. 25/4-28/5/49.**G.**
Str. 7/12/50-20/1/51.**G.**
Str. 17/11-24/12/52.**G.**
Str. 12/4-18/6/55.**G.**
Str. 14/5-11/8/56.**N/C.**

BOILERS:
1578.
4103 *(new)* 27/10/32.
4114 *(new)* 15/3/34.
4124 *(ex8544)* 31/12/35.
4103 *(ex8544)* 14/5/37.
4119 *(ex8516)* 2/11/38.
4100 (ex8557) 10/5/40.

WORKS CODES : Cow - Cowlairs, Dar - Darlington, Don - Doncaster, Ghd - Gateshead, Gor - Gorton, Inv - Inverurie, Str - Stratford.

REPAIR CODES : **C/H** - Casual Heavy, **C/L** - Casual Light, **G** - General, **H** - Heavy, **H/I** - Heavy Intermediate, **L** - Light, **L/I** - Light Intermediate, **N/C** - Not classified.

Home.....8532 and its crew pose for a picture before setting off with a Great Eastern express during the late 1920s

....and away. The same engine, renumbered 61532, passes through Kittybrewster - its home station - during its time with the Great North of Scotland.
Photograph H.C.Casserley.

Part 1 engines in Scotland had boilers which became life-expired during the war, so beginning with 8508 in July 1943 their replacements were to Diagram 25A, which differed by having round-top instead of Belpaire firebox, and a single-plate barrel. Engines so altered then became Part 4 of the class, and by February 1948, nine had been so treated. By that time withdrawal, instead of re-boilering, had then begun, and 1500 (which had only become a Part 4 in November 1947) was withdrawn on June 23rd 1948.

8573 approaches Stratford with a down GE train. Photograph Rail Archive Stephenson.

4107 *(ex8562)* 7/4/42.
4115 *(ex8518)* 17/8/44.
4119 *(ex8580)* 14/5/46.
4101 *(ex1576)* 13/5/47.
4139 *(ex1546)* 28/5/49.
27910 *(ex1568)* 20/1/51.
27905 *(ex1556)* 24/12/52.
27948 *(ex1568)* 18/6/55.

SHEDS:
Gorton.
Stratford 15/10/28.
Colchester 23/5/29.
Stratford 25/9/39.
Colchester 3/12/39.
Ipswich 24/11/44.
Stratford 14/7/46.

RENUMBERED:
1578 10/5/46.
61578 29/5/48.

CONDEMNED:
1/1/57.

8579

Beyer Peacock 6495.

To traffic 25/9/28.

REPAIRS:
Str. 28/1-24/5/29.**L.**
Str. 25/9/30-1/1/31.**G.**
Str. 15/3-27/5/32.**G.** *Reb to part 3.*
Str. 9-14/6/32.**L.**
Str. 11-15/7/32.**N/C.**
Str. 21/9-24/11/33.**G.**
Str. 28/1-22/3/35.**G.**
Str. 2/4-22/5/36.**G.**
Str. 15/11-24/12/37.**G.**
Str. 2-11/2/38.**L.**

Str. 12-26/3/38.**L.**
Str. 22/5-20/7/39.**G.**
Str. 12/2-29/3/41.**G.**
Str. 9-14/9/42.**L.**
Str. 6/5-24/7/43.**G.**
Str. 2-4/3/44.**N/C.**
Str. 1/11-16/12/44.**G.**
Str. 23/3-13/4/46.**L.**
Str. 14/11/46-16/1/47.**G.**
Str. 6/9-8/10/49.**G.**
Str. 30/8-8/9/50.**L.**
Str. 16/8-21/9/51.**G.**
Str. 21/7-18/9/54.**G.**

BOILERS:
1579.
4100 *(new)* 27/5/32.
4115 *(new)* 22/3/35.
4134 *(new)* 22/5/36.
4106 *(ex8509)* 24/12/37.
4122 *(ex8577)* 20/7/39.
4121 *(ex8533)* 29/3/41.
4139 *(ex8553)* 24/7/43.
4160 *(ex8517)* 16/12/44.
4132 *(ex1572)* 16/1/47.
4147 *(ex1525)* 8/10/49.
27930 *(ex1547)* 21/9/51.
27913 *(ex1576)* 18/9/54.

SHEDS:
Gorton.
Stratford 28/1/29.
Colchester 3/6/29.
Ipswich 8/2/31.
Stratford 9/6/32.
Colchester 26/3/39.
Stratford 22/2/41.
Colchester 13/4/41.
Parkeston 12/12/42.
Stratford 22/7/44.
Colchester 9/6/45.
Stratford 20/10/45.
Colchester 18/11/51.

Stratford 13/12/53.

RENUMBERED:
1579 23/3/46.
61579 8/10/49.

CONDEMNED:
1/1/57.

8580

Beyer Peacock 6496.

To traffic 1/10/28.

REPAIRS:
Str. 6/2-17/5/29.**L.**
Str. 29/11/30-6/3/31.**G.**
*Str. 20/7-1/10/32.***G.** *Reb to part 3.*
Str. 25/2-20/3/33.**L.**
Str. 19/4-22/6/34.**G.**
Str. 7/2-19/3/36.**G.**
Str. 27/6-19/8/37.**G.**
Str. 10/1-16/3/39.**G.**
Str. 28/8-22/11/40.**G.**
Str. 20/9-24/10/42.**G.**
Str. 23-27/11/42.**L.**
Str. 4/3-8/5/43.**G.**
Str. 22/2-9/3/44.**N/C.**
Str. 16/12/44-6/1/45.**L.**
Str. 7/10-10/11/45.**G.**
Str. 17/10-26/11/46.**G.**
Str. 19/3-13/5/48.**G.**
Str. 17/2-7/3/49.**C/L.**
Str. 22/10/49-4/3/50.**G.**
Str. 18/3-10/5/52.**G.**
Str. 9/5-19/6/54.**G.**
Str. 3-19/8/54.**C/L.**
Str. 19/7-3/9/55.**C/L.**
Str. 16/10-23/11/56.**C/H.**
Str. 2/9-12/10/57.**G.**
Str. 8-24/4/58.**C/L.**

Str. 24/2/59.*Not repaired.*

BOILERS:
1580.
4102 *(new)* 1/10/32.
4104 *(ex8516)* 22/6/34.
4132 *(new)* 19/3/36.
4148 *(new)* 19/8/37.
4120 *(ex8574)* 16/3/39.
4132 *(ex8538)* 22/11/40.
4119 *(ex8554)* 24/10/42.
4104 *(ex7437)* 10/11/45.
4112 *(ex1537)* 26/11/46.
4151 *(ex1575)* 13/5/48.
4126 *(ex1566)* 4/3/50.
27907 *(ex1564)* 10/5/52.
27917 *(ex1541)* 19/6/54.
27940 *(ex1538)* 12/10/57.

SHEDS:
Gorton.
Stratford 6/2/29.
Parkeston 5/6/29.
Colchester 22/4/31.
Ipswich 9/10/32.
Colchester 6/11/32.
Stratford 20/7/41.
Colchester 10/8/41.
Parkeston 12/12/42.
Stratford 11/11/44.
Colchester 3/9/51.
Stratford 18/11/51.
Grantham 1/2/53.
Cambridge 24/3/57.

RENUMBERED:
1580 16/6/46.
61580 8/5/48.

CONDEMNED:
2/3/59.

7449, formerly 8535, on Stratford shed, 4 August 1945. Photograph H.C.Casserley.

Until a number of the class were sent to Grantham shed, Nottingham (Victoria) was an unusual place to see a B12 - 61565 has just arrived with a local train from Grantham. It was the only one which Stratford managed to put into post-war green, from which it changed to this black BR style when ex-works on March 12th 1949. Its companion 60501 COCK O' THE NORTH was an even more rare visitor to the area.

Photographed on 14 September 1950 at Inverurie, 61504 was taken out of service on June 16th 1950, ending its career a considerable distance from the region for which the locomotive was originally intended.

Double headed trains were uncommon on the Great Eastern and the photographer was fortunate to catch sight of 8503 piloting a 4-4-0 during the early LNER period.

Finally...the first of the class showing enough pipework to satisfy most American railways.